Learner-
Centered
Reform

Dyckman W. Vermilye, EDITOR

1975

CURRENT ISSUES IN HIGHER EDUCATION

ASSOCIATE EDITOR, *William Ferris*

LEARNER-
CENTERED
REFORM

Jossey-Bass Publishers

San Francisco · Washington · London · 1975

LEARNER-CENTERED REFORM
      Dyckman W. Vermilye, Editor

Copyright © 1975 by: American Association for Higher Education

                    Jossey-Bass, Inc., Publishers
                    615 Montgomery Street
                    San Francisco, California 94111

                    Jossey-Bass Limited
                    3 Henrietta Street
                    London WC2E 8LU

Library of Congress Catalogue Card Number LC 75-24001

International Standard Book Number ISBN 0-87589-263-9

Manufactured in the United States of America

JACKET DESIGN BY WILLI BAUM

FIRST EDITION

Code 7516

THE JOSSEY-BASS SERIES IN HIGHER EDUCATION

 A publication of the

AMERICAN ASSOCIATION FOR HIGHER EDUCATION
National Center for Higher Education
One Dupont Circle, Northwest
Washington, D.C. 20036

DYCKMAN W. VERMILYE, *Executive Director*

The American Association for Higher Education, AAHE,
seeks to clarify and help resolve critical issues
in postsecondary education through conferences,
publications, and special projects. Its membership
includes faculty, students, administrators, trustees,
public officials, and interested citizens from all
segments of postsecondary education. This diversity
of membership reflects AAHE's belief that unilateral
solutions to problems are not as sound as those arrived
at through a coming together of all who are affected
by a problem.

Preface

The term *learner-centered reform* seems almost redundant. Is there any other kind of educational reform? People dedicated to the altruistic aims of education do not like to think so. And yet, periodically, concern for the learner gradually changes to concern for the process, which, in turn, changes to a preoccupation with the institution and those who conduct its activities. The idea of learner-centered reform remains, but practice gradually moves away from it.

In the sixties, the higher education community was reminded of how far it had strayed from paying attention to the learner by a complex cultural movement spearheaded for the most part by youthful protesters. Two of the battle cries of that movement, *relevance* and *participatory democracy*, explain much of learner-centered reform. Later, a third cry was added—*accountability*. Together, these words amounted to a charge that institutions had drifted from serving learners to serving the people who worked for the institutions and ran them. Colleges did not meet learning needs as much as they chose students who met their own needs. Out of these charges, the great wave of learner-centered reform was created.

Many of the reforms were not new. Nor was the idea of learner-centered reform. What was new—and probably unprecedented in the educational history of this country—was the magnitude of the reform. Changes that at another time would have been tried on only a small scale at an adventurous institution swept the country: external degrees, open admissions, contract learning, competency-based education, self-paced learning, open universities. At the heart of all these reforms are the learners—not just the traditional eighteen- to twenty-one-year-old college students but virtually all adults in the country. For higher education, the challenges of this large-scale reform and the opportunities that go with it are awe-inspiring.

For a few educators—apparently a growing number—the pace and breadth of reform have inspired not only awe but concern. Their fear, which is not without some basis, is that many good things may have been swept away with the bad as higher education, responding to demands for change, went about the business of putting its own house in order and making a fresh start. While reformers look with pride at the new people entering college programs, the critics look with alarm at what they regard as lowered standards and inflated grades. And as the needs and interests of the learner become increasingly important in shaping the curriculum, some wonder whether colleges and universities are not copping out on their responsibility to lead. And so, it seems, the issues boil down to a crisis of educational leadership: Who, if anyone, will decide the future?

The question is not yet answered, but it will be—and soon. In a sense, higher education is now in a critical shakedown phase. A new philosophy is being tested, and the new programs that embody it are on trial. They are not ideas any longer. They are events. And they are being watched by friends and foes alike. Some will succeed, some not. The big question is whether the philosophy will be successfully put into practice—have we reached the point of no return for traditional higher education?

Institutions of higher learning thus have choices to make. Willard Enteman speaks in this volume of creative planning and contrasts it with what he calls reactive planning—a reflex action that institutions make when they have to. Faced with financial difficulties, many institutions are inclined to pour their current planning energies into developing purely financial strategies for the future. This strategy often amounts to little more than a slowdown in spending and an acceleration in earning. But creative planning, Enteman points out, means choosing positive directions for an institution to take. To make that choice intelligently, critics and supporters of learner-centered reform must begin by resolving their differences frankly and openly, keeping the best interests of the learner in mind. If the differences are not resolved and self-interest prevails, chances are that the planning will be done by others outside the institution. Again, the distinction is between leading and being led.

The chapters of this book were developed from papers presented at the Thirtieth National Conference on Higher Education, held in March 1975. K. Patricia Cross, then president of the American Association for Higher Education, helped in selecting the chapters, along with Stanley Ikenberry, who was chairman of the Conference Planning Committee, and William Ferris of the AAHE staff. My thanks to all of them for their help in determining the form and content of this book.

Washington, D.C.   Dyckman W. Vermilye
September 1975

Contents

Contributors

John G. Bolin, professor of education, Boston College

Howard R. Bowen, Avery professor of economics and education, Claremont Graduate School

Ernest L. Boyer, chancellor, State University of New York

A. Paul Bradley, Jr., director of institutional research, Empire State College, State University of New York

K. Patricia Cross, senior research psychologist, Educational Testing Service, and research educator, Center for Research and Development in Higher Education, University of California, Berkeley

Joseph D. Duffey, general secretary, American Association of University Professors

Willard F. Enteman, provost, Union College

Jerry G. Gaff, director, Center for Professional Development, California State University and Colleges

Harold L. Hodgkinson, director, National Institute of Education, United States Department of Health, Education, and Welfare

Elizabeth H. Johnson, member, Board of Higher Education in Oregon, and chairman, Association of Governing Boards of Universities and Colleges

Morris T. Keeton, provost, Antioch College

Timothy Lehmann, director of program evaluation, Empire State College, State University of New York

Jack Lindquist, research associate for policy analysis, Empire State College, State University of New York

Sylvia G. McCollum, interagency liaison coordinator, education branch, U.S. Bureau of Prisons and Justice Department

L. Richard Meeth, professor of higher education, Department of Higher Education, State University of New York at Buffalo

Victor P. Meskill, vice-president for administration, C. W. Post Center, Long Island University

Robert M. O'Neil, executive vice-president for academic affairs, University of Cincinnati

Carol Van Alstyne, chief economist, Policy Analysis Service, American Council on Education

Jonathan R. Warren, research psychologist, Educational Testing Service

Jacqueline Grennan Wexler, president, Hunter College, City University of New York

Clifton R. Wharton, Jr., president, Michigan State University

Learner-
Centered
Reform

PART ONE

Shaping a
New Tradition

Sooner or later all nontraditional forms of education stop being nontraditional. They become defunct or they become a new tradition. Over the past ten years the various educational approaches that might be included under the term learner-centered reform have moved from the fringes of higher education to the center. They have been tried, analyzed, and challenged. They have not yet passed the testing stage, but they have withstood it well and have grown more vigorous as a result. If learner-centered reform has not yet become established as a new tradition, it has at least demonstrated that it is a serious candidate.

Traditions do not just happen. They spring from an idea. And the idea behind learner-centered reform is, quite simply, that education should be tailored to fit the learner. This idea is a dramatic switch from the traditional expectation that the learner should fit the educational system—should "qualify as college mate-

rial." Translated into principles of motion, the old tradition is that people go to college; the new tradition is that college goes to people. Through such mechanisms as external degrees, contract- and competency-based learning, and personalized instruction, learner-centered reform does send college to people, both figuratively and literally.

The sharp contrast between the old and new traditions has tended to polarize thinking about the proper role of higher education. While some educators are urging the new tradition forward, others are waving red flags over what they believe to be the casualties of the movement. In the opening chapter of this book, Robert M. O'Neil examines this polarity and contends that the critics of learner-centered reform deserve better answers than they have been getting. These critics, he points out, include some of the most respected scholars in the country, and their concerns—which stem from lowered admissions requirements, lowered standards, inflated grades, quotas for students and faculty, and curtailed research—should not be dismissed offhandedly. Suggesting the kinds of responses needed if "the anxiety that now jeopardizes learner-centered reform" is to be reduced, O'Neil gives us reason to hope that the traditional and nontraditional philosophies may not be as irreconcilable as the current debate implies.

Believing, perhaps, that the best way to establish a new tradition is to advance it, Ernest L. Boyer and Jacqueline Wexler call for stepped-up efforts to bring learning to the people. For Boyer, who is chancellor of the State University of New York, one way to do this is to overhaul the educational time sequence—or, at least, to consider seriously whether present time structures, rooted in the past, are the best way to organize learning. Boyer criticizes the rigidity of educational time blocks, noting the poor articulation between college and secondary school on the one hand and college and adult life styles on the other. He also questions the overall length of formal learning. If education is to be truly learner-centered, he argues, then breaking the time barrier should be one of the first items on the reform agenda.

Wexler, president of Hunter College, perceives another kind of barrier, one that is psychological rather than chronological. She contends that the persistence of a hierarchical philosophy is thwarting efforts to distribute educational opportunities fairly. Aspirations embodied in such a phrase as "the best and the bright-

est" still dominate the thinking of many who teach and many who learn, she says. Educational justice and quality are the professed goals, but they are not likely to be realized until the country genuinely reorders its values.

A third barrier, bureaucratic red tape, is described by Morris Keeton, provost of Antioch College. He looks at some of the specific regulations that make survival difficult for nontraditional programs or that discourage their creation. For Keeton, the question is not whether red tape is bad—sometimes, he points out, it has a positive effect—but whether "interference can be held to a socially useful level." He reviews a number of state approval and eligibility regulations that inhibit reform and glances briefly at the accreditation problems experienced by innovative programs.

In the final chapter of Part One, Elizabeth H. Johnson examines a major source of the regulations described by Keeton: statewide governing or coordinating agencies. A member of the Oregon Board of Higher Education, Johnson traces the growth and evolution of state boards and offers a number of arguments for strengthening their role as regulatory agencies. She maintains that many of the fears and uncertainties institutions have about loss of autonomy and academic freedom would subside if the role and functions of state boards were clearly defined.

The chapters in this part reflect a common concern: that of shaping learner-centered reform into a new tradition for higher education. Whether the nontraditional becomes the new tradition will depend largely on how reform-minded educators react to barriers such as those described by the authors. Perhaps, as O'Neil suggests, the best strategy is not to swing around them or vault over them, or even to break through them, but to work creatively and rationally toward removing them.

William Ferris

1

Pros and Cons of Learner-Centered Reform

Robert M. O'Neil

🌾🌾🌾🌾🌾🌾🌾

Learner-centered reform is in difficulty, not only in this country but abroad as well. Take, for example, the controversy at the Vincennes branch of the University of Paris. Opened shortly after the student uprising of the late 1960s, this campus was designed to provide nontraditional learning opportunities to working class youth. Enrollment grew rapidly, partly because students who could not pass the difficult French baccalaureate exams were admitted. Although the curriculum was rather eclectic, and apparently quite popular with the students, the Ministry of Education disapproved of the new campus. In November 1974, the Ministry ordered Vincennes to stop awarding two-year degrees to students who entered without passing the baccalaureate exam, but the university refused to comply. Three months later a French magazine carried a sensational story about a course in "sexology" which featured slides from the San Francisco International Museum of Erotic Art. The magazine article was followed quickly by a national television expose of the course. At this point, the Ministry announced that the course was being "suspended"—even though it was being offered on a noncredit basis anyway.

The Vincennes incident may sound remote to those concerned about learner-centered reform in the United States, but there are striking parallels—both in the vulnerability of nontraditional curricula and in the critics' tendency to dismiss *all* nontraditional educational trends, whether good or bad. The Vincennes problem is, in fact, quite close to home, even if the American scenario is slightly different.

Although learner-centered reforms have been supported by federal agencies and national foundations, they have fared less well with the higher education establishment in Cambridge, New Haven, Palo Alto, Hyde Park in Chicago, and Morningside Heights. It is from these centers of learning that the harshest criticism has recently come. Let me give a few examples. In spring 1974, Yale historian C. Van Woodward addressed some seventy senior scholars at a conference sponsored by the International Council on the Future of the University. Woodward lamented certain recent trends—inflation of grades, relaxation or abandonment of language and other requirements—and then, significantly, he warned: "We have seen the curriculum trivialized and vulgarized and made relevant, and these [trends] are part of the legacy of the late 1960s." Note the juxtaposition of phenomena made by a profound and sensitive scholar: making the curriculum "relevant" is linked with making it "trivial" and "vulgar."

Nearly a year later, a double issue of *Daedalus* served as a final report for the Assembly on University Goals and Governance. Having been counsel to the assembly in its initial years, I take its conclusions quite seriously. The theme of the *Daedalus* report was "American Higher Education: Toward an Uncertain Future." Let me cite three alarming passages from the eighty-some essays by major scholars and university administrators. First there is a warning by Columbia University philosopher Charles Frankel: "Consider the following phenomena: grade inflation, the progressive elimination of foreign language requirements from the curricula, the steady dilution of even mild distribution requirements, the regularity with which curricula reforms turn out to involve simply less reading and writing, the living conditions in dormitories from which universities have almost entirely withdrawn their supervisory authority although they continue to pay the bills, the double talk about quotas that are not quotas and *apartheid* that is not *apartheid.*"[1]

Gordon Craig, chairman of the history department at Stanford, echoes Frankel's concern: "The insistence of the young, during the late 1960s, that the university establishment did not understand them and their world found an all too eager agreement on the part of faculty members who should have known better. Suddenly the cry of relevance filled the land; curricular requirements were heedlessly jettisoned because someone said that they prevented the investigation of the real problems that confronted our society. We entered the age of the Green Stamp University, in which the student receives the same number of stamps for a course on Bay Area pollution or human sexuality as he does for American history or the Greek philosophers, sticks them happily into his book, and gets a diploma when it is filled. Whether he has received an education in the course of all this is doubtful."[2]

Finally, there is this comment from Allan Bloom, an American-trained political scientist now teaching at the University of Toronto: "Connected with [the] new radical egalitarianism in the university were the abandonment of requirements, the demand for student participation in all functions of the university, the evaluation of professors by students, sex counseling, the renouncing of standards because they encourage discrimination and unhealthy competition, a continuing inflation of grades, concentration on teaching rather than scholarship, open admissions, the introduction of new programs to fit every wish, and quotas in the admission of students and the hiring of faculty. It is questionable

---

[1] Charles Frankel, "Reflections on a Worn-Out Model," *Daedalus*, Fall 1974, p. 25.
[2] Gordon A. Craig, "Green Stamp or Structured Undergraduate Education," *Daedalus*, Fall 1974, p. 144.

whether a university can pursue its proper end if it must be engaged in the fight against social inequality."[3]

All four of these critics—Woodward, Frankel, Craig, and Bloom—tend to connect many diverse trends they dislike and perhaps fear. By implication, learner-centered reform becomes either the cause or the consequence of inflated grades, lowered admission requirements, affirmative action, elimination of language and other requirements, student evaluation of teaching, abandonment of research, and many other ills that afflict the contemporary academy. If one seeks a scapegoat for what is wrong with higher education, reform appears to be a vulnerable candidate.

Obviously, there are many ways one could answer the critics. One could argue, for example, that most of the reforms scorned by these scholars are not new ones. They have occurred in traditional curricula at traditional universities, and many have been accepted by otherwise conservative faculties. In fact, non-traditional options existed long before there was a Minnesota Metro, an Empire State, or a Ferris State. The Harvard Junior Fellow program is a notable example. Its popularity in the 1930s explains why such scholars as McGeorge Bundy and Arthur Schlesinger, Jr., hold no earned graduate degrees. One could also point to the Yale Scholars of the House program, which allowed seniors in the early 1950s to pursue independent study for a full semester of credit without any formal course requirements. One could especially remind critics of Robert Hutchins' curriculum at the University of Chicago.

In relation to student evaluation of teaching, a subject of much contemporary concern in traditional academic circles, we find that it is not a recent innovation either. At least twenty-five years ago, the *Harvard Crimson* Confidential Guide was well established (and generally accepted by the faculty) as a student rating survey. A decade later it was followed by the Berkeley *Slate Supplement*. Although these examples are drawn from highly selective institutions, the principle is clear: Learner-centered reform is not simply a product of the student disorder of the late 1960s or the malaise of the 1970s.

[3] Allan Bloom, "The Failure of the University," *Daedalus*, Fall 1974, p. 64.

Given that many aspects of learner-centered reform are not recent innovations, the intensity of current attack is all the more surprising. We must probe deeper for explanations. Paradoxically, it may be that criticism from traditionalists reflects both the limitations and the triumphs of learner-centered reform. On one hand, the critics are genuinely perplexed by what they see—and with some justification. Yet at the same time, because they see some good in the movement, they may wish they could play a greater role in it. Learner-centered reform is both alluring and somewhat frightening to professors who have devoted their lives to laboratory research and fifty-minute lectures.

Some problems of learner-centered reform have resulted from its very successes. The traditionalists may be a bit envious of the attention nontraditional programs are getting from major foundations and such federal agencies as the Fund for the Improvement of Postsecondary Education. Success in attacting students also causes problems. Because enrollments are rising at the nontraditional campuses, critics suspect that these programs are attracting students who might otherwise be enrolled in traditional programs. Much of the harshest criticism comes from those disciplines in which enrollment declines have been most marked. Many study areas have been affected, but changing student interest has had a particularly acute impact on modern languages. (A recent survey taken by the Modern Language Association reports that fewer and fewer colleges and universities require foreign language study: down from 88.9 percent in 1965 to 56 percent in fall 1974.)

The sense of competition may be largely illusory, however. Although Empire State draws some students away from Columbia and NYU, applications at both these institutions have risen; Minnesota Metro has not grown at the expense of either the University of Minnesota or Macalester; and Ferris State does not undercut either Western Michigan or Kalamazoo. We have no accurate national data, unfortunately, but it is a fair guess that most students attending truly nontraditional institutions probably would not be enrolled at all if only the traditional options existed. Even at traditional campuses, the institution of innovative and learner-centered curricula has probably helped to increase or stabilize enrollments. The steady growth of part-time students at most major universities demonstrates the value of flexible options for the established as well as the new sectors.

Some aspects of learner-centered reform are not always defensible, of course. Several developments appear to validate the harshest criticism. Few actions could have done more harm to the public reputation and stature of learner-centered reform than the academic scandals at Lincoln Open University and the School of Education at the University of Massachusetts, Amherst. While these two incidents could be dismissed as more bizarre than representative, the institutions and people involved in them had played major parts in the recent reform movement. Such incidents make much more difficult the task of convincing not only the skeptics but also the uncommitted that nontraditional programs are still respectable.

The consumer protection movement, which has recently spilled over into higher education, also focuses attention on some of the shortcomings of nontraditional programs. While the initial targets are marginal vocational schools and proprietary institutions that have lured students with exaggerated claims, there is growing concern also about external and nontraditional degree programs. George Arnstein, executive director of the National Advisory Council on Education Professions Development, has recently pointed out that "legitimate ventures such as a 'university without walls' can in many cases look uncomfortably like a diploma mill."[4] Meanwhile, several state governments are taking a close look at external degree programs that are run by out-of-state institutions. Sometimes there is little contact with, or supervision by, the parent organization, which may have marginal status even at home. Coordinating boards in New York, Texas, Minnesota, and Ohio, among others, have begun to impose tighter controls on nonresident institutions offering courses and degrees to their residents. The motives of such agencies may not be entirely pure, obviously, and their concern may not be solely qualitative. In a time of increasing competition for students, incursions by out-of-state institutions, regardless of their academic standing, clearly threaten local colleges and universities fighting for survival.

Accreditation is another problem. So far, several of the

[4]George Arnstein, "Ph.D., Anyone?" *American Education,* July 1974.

regional associations have been receptive to external degrees. North Central has recently accredited the graduate degrees of the Union of Experimenting Colleges and Universities, and earlier gave its blessing to such institutions as Minnesota Metro, Governors State, and Sangamon State. The Southern Regional Association has reformulated some of its accrediting standards after surveying nontraditional programs at member institutions. The Federation of Regional Accrediting Commissions two years ago developed and widely circulated an "Interim Statement on Accreditation and Nontraditional Study," which gave impetus to developments nationally. But the role of the professional and specialized accrediting bodies remains uncertain. As the report of the Commission on Non-Traditional Study warned: "Their work is heavily guided by reliance on structural and operational standards; many of them are highly specific, and some of them seem to outsiders to be incapable of defense on any rational basis. . . . To such agencies, the idea of nontraditional study and particularly of the external degree is likely to appear to be the reemergence of an old enemy."[5]

The threat posed by learner-centered reform to scholars and teachers of the traditional mold is a genuine one. If the influence of the learner in shaping the curriculum and evaluating his performance expands, it may be at the expense of the instructor. The authority of the faculty member in the teaching-learning relationship—already shaken by grading reforms, abolition of requirements, and relaxed class attendance rules—may seem to be undermined even more severely by the newer reforms. If the results of the new programs lack consistency, and in some cases lack even academic substance, the dismay of the senior professoriate is not surprising. As nontraditional programs expand, excesses and abuses are bound to occur, or at least be visible, more often than in traditional programs. Maintaining standards is harder in external and competency-based programs than in fifty-minute classes with papers, exams, and quarterly grades. Thus, there is some substance to what Craig, Woodward, Frankel, and Bloom are saying about the erosion not only of values but of academic authority as well.

There must be ways of meeting such criticism more effec-

[5] Commission on Non-Traditional Study, *Diversity by Design* (San Francisco: Jossey-Bass, 1973).

tively than has been done to date. We should at least be able to persuade conscientious critics that higher grades, lower standards, student apathy, and faculty malaise cannot all fairly be attributed to curricular innovation. I would like to suggest several steps that might be taken to reduce the anxiety that now jeopardizes learner-centered reform.

Several approaches might be taken at the individual college or campus. One positive step would be to integrate the nontraditional units and programs more fully into the total fabric of the institution than they now are. Such programs have often been isolated, both geographically and administratively, from the campus center. As a result, nontraditional thinking fails to reach the bulk of the faculty, who may be discouraged from innovating by the thought that "we already have an experimental college" or "the extension division grants experiential credit."

For similar reasons, rather than confining institutional support of reform to already committed colleges or departments, it would be helpful if administrations provided even modest support for innovative programs within traditional units. New experiential or competency-based options in colleges of arts and sciences would be possibilities. Administrators at traditional campuses could do much to foster understanding of nontraditional curricula, allay fears, and correct misconceptions by sponsoring faculty forums that would welcome traditionalists as well as innovators. Such forums could provide the bridge that is now clearly and sorely lacking. In addition, learner-centered reform in the traditional fields most threatened by enrollment declines and shifting student demands could have positive results. In my own institution, the University of Cincinnati, our foreign language departments began to work with the College of Business Administration two years ago to develop a most imaginative international business program. This program meets a growing demand, which is reflected in strong student interest. As a result of this and similar innovations, our modern language requirement has survived, and the enrollment in upper division language courses has increased.

When we shift our focus from the campus to the region, we find that the potential of consortia and other interinstitutional arrangements for facilitating nontraditional study has barely been tapped. At one level, there is the model of an interinstitutional degree such as that offered by the Union of Experimenting Colleges and Universities. But consortia may aid learner-centered reform in other ways as well. As student interests change, a group of institutions can respond to such changes far better and with far less internal dislocation than can a single campus. The opportunities for curricular enrichment through cross-registration and exchange of faculty offer more flexibility in meeting student needs than any one institution can muster. For example, the greater Cincinnati Consortium is now developing multi-institutional options in women's studies, Asian studies, gerontology, and Judaic studies. No one member of the consortium could muster such strength alone, but working together they have been able to offer a rich variety of complementary courses.

Consortia also distribute and thus minimize the costs of responding to new student demands and interests. A consortium-based media center or broadcasting facility may be feasible when no single institution can shoulder the cost alone. If student interest in the field lags, all members of the consortium share the consequences; perhaps, by working together, they can find an alternative use for the equipment or facility. Thus, interinstitutional collaboration might appear to be one solution to the shortcomings of learner-centered reforms. Unfortunately, however, some critics are no more sanguine about interinstitutional cooperation than about nontraditional programs.

Local and regional solutions are not sufficient however. The major missionary work must be done at the national level. As a first step, we need to define and explain the available models for learner-centered reform more clearly than we have so far. Even granting that educational innovation must be eclectic and result-oriented, there does seem to have been too much doing and not enough thinking in these past few years. We are fortunate to have had the views of the Commission on Non-Traditional Study. But we need more such analysis and evaluation, and we need it in a form that will make clearer to traditional faculties the potential for creative teaching and research. Distrust and anxiety must be dealt with directly and with reasoned, careful, and scholarly responses of a kind that have been too rare in the past.

Those who are committed to the cause of learner-centered reform have tended to talk too much to themselves and not enough to those who are fearful, skeptical, or simply ignorant about nontraditional programs. The annual meetings of higher education associations might provide a forum for dialogue between these groups, rather than simply for reaffirmation among the faithful. As advocates of learner-centered reform, we must hear the critics' concerns firsthand. Then, it is essential that we respond both defensively and constructively to the criticisms that divide the two major academic camps.

Work at the national level should also extend to the accrediting associations—not merely to the groups that have been receptive, but also to the specialized, professional, and disciplinary organizations that have far less sympathy. Such groups must be reached before attitudes harden and boundaries are demarcated in ways that may take decades to soften. Frankel, Woodward, Craig, and Bloom are not alone. Nor are they in error in some of their criticisms. They are genuinely concerned and alarmed about developments they believe will be deeply detrimental to American higher education as they value it. They need and deserve better answers than they have received.

2

Changing Time Requirements

Ernest L. Boyer

A most unusual paradox exists in higher education. On the one hand, we are sure that people learn at different rates. On the other hand, one of the few generalizations we can make about a college baccalaureate degree is that it usually takes four years. In the area where people are most flexible, our educational structure is most rigid.

Curiously, there is nothing quite so sacred in American education as established time blocks. Eight years of lower schooling and four years of high school are followed by four years of higher learning. This sequence has been rigidly maintained and now has sainthood status. In the bulging bag of education literature, no work explores in depth the amount of time young people should spend in elementary school, high school, and college. That the educational time schedule should be uniform for all students is one of the most unchallenged assumptions about learning in the United States today.

Our failure to ask questions about the length of learning time is doubly curious because our present structure occurred by accident, not design. The four-year BA degree began at Harvard because many of the founders and early leaders of Harvard were educated at Cambridge University. In the early 1600s, Cambridge had three academic terms, and undergraduates began college between the ages of twelve and fifteen; the college program normally lasted four years. It was quite predictable, as Samuel Eliot Morison writes in *Founding of Harvard College,* that Harvard would merely imitate the Cambridge model. Harvard College opened with three terms, admitted students aged twelve to fifteen, instituted a prescribed curriculum (as late as 1854, Harvard College allowed its students only two electives), and the four-year model became the norm.

All eighteen colleges established in America before 1800 simply imitated the Harvard four-year program. In fact, it was not until 1819 that the University of Virginia attempted a scheme that was more indigenously American. Although it also had a four-year program, the number of terms was reduced from three to two in a daring innovation so young men could be at home during planting and harvesting times.

When the midwestern state universities were founded in the mid-nineteenth century, they merely imitated the eastern colleges. Everyone constructed four-year undergraduate programs, but they also cut the school year to two terms each so the youngsters could go home to help with the crops.

Ironically, even as American colleges were imitating Cambridge and Oxford programs, the latter were in the midst of an educational revolution. English colleges were to change considerably by the late seventeenth century, and undergraduate years at Cambridge and Oxford were reduced from four to three; the three-year program remains to this day.

From time to time, a few college presidents did suggest a varied schedule. President Francis Wayland of Brown University, for example, wrote in 1850, "It is the design of the Corporation to require for the degree of Bachelor of Arts and of Philosophy, an amount of study which may be accomplished in three years, but which may, if he pleases, occupy the student profitably for four years."[1] Wayland's flexible new design never saw the light of day, however. But then, around the turn of the century, Nicholas Murray Butler, Charles W. Eliot, and William Rainey Harper tried to shake up the academic world. They felt compelled to do so because of startling new and dramatic trends. First, high school had come along. Second, the length of law and medical school programs had increased from two to four years. Third, the professional schools insisted that students have college degrees before they could be enrolled.

The academic turf was beginning to get far too crowded. In early days, American students went to school between the ages of eight and fifteen. They attended a Latin school, an English grammar school, or an academy. Only one boy in three hundred went to college. But after the Civil War, the private academies gradually gave way to the new public high schools; and these schools, feeling their oats, imposed a four-year program on top of the primary schools. And the primary schools, not to be outdone, swiftly puffed up their programs to seven or eight years in imitation of the waning academies.

And so what had once been seven or eight years of precollege study had suddenly become twelve. As a result, colleges that had once admitted pink-cheeked sixteen-year-olds suddenly found themselves confronting sideburned, mustachioed freshmen of nineteen or twenty years of age. Eliot became alarmed, and, in a speech to the National Education Association, he fumed: "The average age of admission to Harvard College . . . has now reached the extravagant limit of eighteen years and ten months. Harvard College is not at all peculiar in this respect; indeed, many of the country colleges find their young men older still at entrance. . . . The average college graduate who fits himself well for any one of the learned professions, including teaching, can hardly begin to support himself until he is twenty-seven years old."[2] Parenthetically, the average life expectancy for white males in 1890 was about forty-six years.

[1]Walter C. Bronson, *The History of Brown University, 1765-1914* (Providence, R.I.: Brown University Press, 1914), p. 281.
[2]*Education Reform: Essays and Addresses* (New York. Century, 1909), p. 151.

How was the structure to be changed? Eliot of Harvard and Butler of Columbia, sometimes working in collusion, decided on a two-pronged remedy. First, they tried to push high school work down into the scandalously wasteful adolescent years so that students could finish high school at age sixteen or seventeen. They tried to do this through the famous NEA-sponsored "Report of the Committee of Ten," released in 1893. The committee was chaired by Eliot. The report, one of the most influential documents of American educational history, urged, among other things, that "the secondary school period should be made to begin two years earlier than at present, leaving six years instead of eight for the elementary school period." The secondary schools eventually did admit students earlier, but the primary schools refused to give up their eight-year time block. Instead, they simply added two years of extra work at the beginning, admitting youngsters at five or six years of age.

The other prong of the Eliot-Butler push was to shorten the number of college years. In his 1902 annual report, Butler wrote, "Four years is . . . too long a time to devote to the college course as now constituted, especially for students who are to remain in university residence as technical or professional students." By 1905, he had convinced his faculty to adopt "a professional option" plan whereby, after two or three years at Columbia College, a student might go on directly to one of the professional schools of the university. The plan attracted only a few students each year until it was virtually abolished in 1953.

Eliot, meanwhile, had persuaded his reluctant faculty to abandon the four-year residency degree in 1902. Eliot's clinching argument was that perhaps one-fourth of the undergraduates were already completing their basic requirements in three years and that many lazy and unambitious young men at Harvard seemed to "prefer a residence of four years, chiefly for social or athletic considerations." By 1906, 41 percent of Harvard College students graduated in three or three and one-half years. As many as 25 percent of the students graduated in that length of time until after World War I, when the baccalaureate slid back into "normalcy"—which seemed quite appropriate for the America of Calvin Coolidge.

During the 1890s, Harper advocated a different approach at the University of Chicago. He suggested that high school begin in the eighth grade and end at the eleventh, with two years of "junior college" work for students sixteen to eighteen years old either at a high school or college. Thus, when the University of Chicago opened in 1892, it offered a two-year unit officially named a junior college and an upper two-year unit called university college. Harper helped give birth to the junior college movement through encouraging high schools to offer lower collegiate courses.

Harper's idea of an intermediate collegiate institution did not take hold. However, when Robert M. Hutchins became president of the University of Chicago in 1929, he revived the idea of an intermediate college comprising the last two years of secondary school and the first two years of college. Chicago awarded BA degrees between 1937 and 1950 to numerous eighteen- and nineteen-year-old students who attended the intermediate college. But this early-college school was no more popular than Harper's institution.

These attacks on the time structure of education seem to have lasted just about as long as the giants who led them. I suspect that the rationale of educators might have been, "if Harvard, Columbia, and Chicago can't change something, it's best to conclude that it can't be changed."

During the mid-1950s foundations pushed for a flexible time schedule. The most publicized was the early admission program. Under this plan, twelve colleges and universities, including Yale, Columbia, Fisk, and Utah, admitted gifted students after their third high school year, thus reducing the total high school-college time block from eight to seven years. However, most colleges were so hung up about the age-bracketing of students that several babied their fifteen-year-old "early admits," to the point that one would have thought they were neurotic hemophiliacs instead of normal boys and girls who were slightly younger than their classmates. Of the 1350 students admitted early to college between 1951 and 1955, most did as well as, or better, academically than their older classmates.

Nonetheless, the program died. Colleges were not that interested, and many high schools genuinely resisted the program. One principal told a college official, "We don't like the idea of the colleges taking our leaders out of high school at the end of the tenth or eleventh grade." It was the system, not the student, that ruled the day!

Why have we been so unsuccessful in our search for a learner-centered time structure for American education? There is inertia, and there is institutional rigidity as well. But responsible objections have also been voiced. For one thing, student and faculty response is definitely mixed. Although the idea of flexible time is now welcomed by many older students, younger students—particularly those from the upper-middle class—are lukewarm or even hostile. "We like college and its social life," the argument seems to run. "Why should we be asked to shorten this stage of life when we find it so pleasurable and rewarding?" Faculty members with whom I have talked are generally sympathetic to flexible time. But they are also wary, quite understandably calculating what effect it might have on the requirements they have carefully devised over the years for majors in their discipline.

Critics also challenge the idea of reducing the prework time span of American education on grounds of public policy. Such a move, they contend, would flood the labor market with young people and swell the ranks of the jobless at a time when the country is already plagued by unemployment. "Let the kids stay in college for as long as possible," this *Realpolitik* analysis runs, "because we really don't want them competing for jobs any sooner than necessary." From this viewpoint, the college degree becomes a kind of immigration barrier set up to restrain, at least temporarily, a surge of unwanted labor competition.

Finally, and perhaps most cogently, we have the "knowledge explosion" proposition. The sheer volume of what should be learned is growing every year. Even the most impressionistic evidence drives home the point. In 1948, the year Harry Truman defeated Thomas Dewey, the *New York Times Index* ran to 1211 pages; by 1970, the total had soared to 2291 pages. Over 2000 large, closely printed pages are now required merely to list, by author, title, and subject, the paperback books currently in print. *Dissertations in Progress, Scholarly Books in America,* and *Reader's Guide to Periodical Literature* are similarly swollen. Although the heft of the *Times* and the volume of dissertations in progress are hardly precise guides to the state of human knowledge, they do indicate something of what confronts the individual who wants to learn.

What options do we have? Should we simply tack more and more years onto formal education? That hardly seems feasible.

The body of new knowledge has grown so dramatically that one person could not begin to cover all the subjects even if the undergraduate curriculum were extended to twenty years. To assume that it can all be acquired in four prework years is utter nonsense. In 1868, John Stuart Mill defined the baccalaureate degree as "the mastery of the body of knowledge that mankind had achieved up to that time." I doubt that anyone accepts that as a working definition in 1975. Further, occupational and career changes and shifts in intellectual disciplines are occurring so rapidly that no college program—no matter how ingenious—can possibly prepare all college students completely for life, work, and leisure.

I believe we are beginning to understand that our formal learning schedule must consider, and be balanced by, people's needs to feel useful, loved, active, or engaged. Charles Fourier, the nineteenth-century French socialist, once said that everyone has a *papillon*, or butterfly, drive, a need to flit about and to vary routines and activities. Humans, to Fourier, were not made to sit passively or do just one thing for a lifetime or even a decade. Bertrand Russell considered "boredom as a powerful factor in human behavior." In my opinion, that statement has received far less attention than it deserves. How many persons could or should endure twenty or so years of unrelieved classroom study, no matter how urgent intellectual or cultural matters are? To impose this on individuals during their most vigorous, athletic, questing years seems only to invite Dostoevskian revolts and antisocial outbursts.

Where do we go from here? I do not believe we should call for less education, but rather I suggest that the sequence might be reordered. One approach would be to shorten or interrupt the sixteen prebaccalaureate years and lengthen the students' post-BA education. The notion that education is something one gets only before going to work must be replaced with the idea that education is a lifelong process, going on during, after, and in between working days. If we can change the idea, our colleges will increasingly move from serving the calendar to serving people of all ages. Education would then be truly learner-centered.

Changing educators' assumptions about the appropriate time sequence will not be easy. American education is presently a giant layer cake, and each layer—nursery school, elementary school, high school, college, and professional school—is separated from the others by the icing of tradition. Perhaps the time has come for a national commission, comprised of representatives from education at every level, to examine the timing of American education—not just high school education or college education but the whole sequence of learning to which we subject our students. Certainly the time has come for us at least to challenge the rigid set of time requirements that have evolved by chance and survived by inertia and that are hardly learner-centered in their length or pattern.

Exhilaration is notably lacking in higher education today. Financially and intellectually, the university world seems to be declining in importance. But although some of the old patterns may be crumbling, if we could only liberate our imaginations we could well be on the verge of one of the most creative and rewarding periods of education.

During the 1950s and 1960s, we put up new buildings with brick and mortar to handle the flood of new students. During the 1970s and 1980s, we need to think carefully of our inner structure and design. It will not be easy. Sloppy standards are perils, and so are the losses of vital human connections that make learning so exciting. Flexibility can sometimes be confused with doing your own thing; and there is a danger in changing for change's sake, or in changing to conform to a new fad. Careless innovation is as much a threat as smugly standing pat. As Ralph Waldo Emerson once warned, "A great licentiousness treads on the heels of reformation." Under no circumstances must we let our American system of colleges and universities, which C. P. Snow has called "one of the world's great glories," decline in quality.

But neither can we afford to ignore the fact that increasing numbers of adults want to learn more about something. According to a recent ETS survey, "among people 25 or older, there are 15 million college graduates, many of them ready for further professional training or intellectual development. There are also 71 million high school graduates who either never started or never finished college. Some 25 million people in this age group are already continuing their education on a part-time basis, but fewer than one in nine of them attends a college or university."[3] Higher education must seek ways to serve the special needs of these

---

[3] Pamela Roelfs, "Teaching and Counseling Older College Students," *Findings*, 2(1), 5.

potential students. We are now a learning society, struggling to stay abreast of knowledge explosions and cataclysmic world changes. Our universities simply cannot afford to remain ghettos for youth, structured to serve the needs of an earlier civilization. We have no alternative but to adjust responsibly—no matter how painful it may be.

Alfred North Whitehead once wrote, "It is the first step of wisdom to recognize that the major changes of civilization are processes which all but wreck society." I believe that we are now going through a profound change in our society. But I am equally convinced of two other things. One is that the wrenches we are going through in higher education will help rebuild, not wreck, the fabric of American life. The other is that this is one of the great historical times to be involved in education. This may seem strange to say, given our grave fiscal problems. But higher education has almost always been short of cash. Seldom, however, have American universities been given a greater opportunity to examine their priorities and students' needs. I find this a most exciting prospect.

3

Educating a
Whole People

Jacqueline Grennan Wexler

For the past two decades, I have been preoccupied personally and professionally in trying to understand the role of the individual in shaping his or her life in relation to society. Raised and rooted in an Illinois farm community, I continue to respect what I have come to call " the statistical wisdom of the whole people." In a limited, even provincial world, such "whole" people seem to exercise more power over their personal destinies than do the sons and daughters of socially prominent or financially successful parents—the so-called "best" people. In no way do I intend to put down initiative, ambition, expertise, or achievement. Rather, I would like to consider what initiative, ambition, expertise, and achievement might mean to individuals in a world that respected distributive quality rather than hierarchical success.

23

Shortly after I had finished reading Halberstam's *The Best and the Brightest* a few years ago, I met an old friend, Fred Burkhardt. I informed him that, if my memory was correct, he was the only person I dealt with in Washington during the 1960s who never used phrases like "the best people." He said he hoped my memory was indeed accurate and attributed his attitude to the Al Smith liberal tradition. In that context, he quoted Smith as having once said, "The best people should always be on tap, but never on top." The phrase rings true as I wrestle with the problems created by a world characterized more and more by sophisticated knowl edge and narrow professionalism.

The academic world is, of necessity, a world of professionalism and expertise. The scholars in each discipline form a kind of high priesthood to outside lay people—even though they remain a collegium of researchers trying to learn, to master what nobody yet has been able to teach. Any field of expertise expands until it is forced to divide. Division is necessary not only to allow the researcher to master the area of his or her sophisticated concern but also to allow that person to maintain a position of preeminence in the eyes of peers, students, and the general public.

The "best" colleges and universities have always seen themselves as competing for the "best" faculties. These faculties have competed for the "best" students to use as intellectual apprentices in their continuing research and to educate in their own particular traditions. The benefits of such traditions are obvious in the achievements of the pure sciences, of the social sciences, of literary scholarship, and of medicine. We can no longer imagine a world without the continuing development of a scholarly research tradition. It is a necessary condition for the fullest possible life of the whole people. In that sense, the scholars and researchers—"the best and the brightest" of the intellectual elite—are actually the servants and the ministers, rather than the priests of the whole people, performing for the world one of the most necessary life functions.

If we were to take, for example, the Harvard faculty and the Harvard curriculum and expand them exponentially, would we not have arrived at utopia for the whole people? I suspect that the Harvard faculty would be the first to reject this kind of utopia. They and their colleagues in comparable institutions—if indeed any other institution would call itself comparable—have defined their teaching mission by their admissions criteria. For generations they have sought, nurtured, and sent forth the men (and recently a few women) whom Halberstam describes with both admiration and disdain as "the best and the brightest." The intellectual stimulation and the challenge to national and world leadership of those students have made their mark. The world would in countless ways be poorer if Harvard did not exist. At the same time, it is foolish to expect that persons educated and reinforced in that kind of an environment have much sensitivity, empathy, or even understanding for the people they dream of leading one day.

Educating a whole people is a tricky business. Educating a whole people in a nation committed to free speech and to a legislated tax-base is even trickier. Experts in any field expect to form the neophyte in their own tradition. The free society, which both respects them for their expertise and refuses to accept them as a power elite, must decide to what extent they will support their research and the ways in which their expertise can be made available to the broad-based population.

American higher education in this century has been almost schizophrenic in its development. As knowledge and wealth began to spread more distributively across the populace, people began to ask, and then to demand, that their children have more equitable access to the world of the privileged. Education and privilege have been highly correlated for some time now. College catalogues have stressed the dignity of the liberally educated person, the man or woman educated for life rather than for making a living. But those in higher education were pleased when studies demonstrated the differential in earning expectancies between the educationally privileged and the educationally disadvantaged. It had been disheartening for educators to realize that the bargaining power of plumbers, welders, firemen, truck drivers, and sanitation engineers had achieved for them a material standard of living equal to or greater than that of many teachers. Today, greater access to higher education is forcing recruiters and curricula planners to be more honest about liberal and career possibilities. If ten candidates are clearly able to perform one available professional task, nine may find it difficult to adjust to less-favored employment while they contemplate the wholeness of their liberally educated selves.

To the extent that higher education in the past has conditioned, even though inadvertently, the whole society to a purely hierarchical notion of dignity, it has, I believe, engineered a cruel joke on that society. Upward mobility ladders are attractive until there is no room on such narrow rungs for the increasing numbers who might try to climb higher. The oversupply of Ph.D.s who compete for the few available teaching positions in our institutions are current players in that drama of frustration, as are the seven to ten able students who compete for every available admissions slot in our medical schools. The academic world has long been a major critic of the cut-throat competition of organized sports and of many big businesses, where only a few can win the prize. Yet, ironically, academics have inferred, if not directly stated, to students that the most desirable lifestyle was that formed in their own image. Those who failed or chose not to achieve this were dropouts from the educational system. The results of this conditioning are beginning to confront us on all sides. The oversupply of trained, able, and motivated persons for many positions is obvious. The undersupply of trained, able, and motivated persons for the production of needed goods and needed services is also obvious.

As a trustee of the University of Pennsylvania, I recently listened to a briefing by the dean of the medical school. Citing data from the National Center for Health Statistics, he outlined the percentage trends for the supply of active doctors by specialty. General practitioners comprised 50 percent of the active medical profession in 1949, 22 percent in 1970, and will be 11 percent in 1980. Medical specialists represented 11 percent in 1949 and are projected to be 26 percent in 1980. During the same period, the number of surgeons will have risen from 17 percent to 31 percent; and, perhaps most significantly, research medicine will preoccupy 32 percent of the medical profession in 1980 as compared to less than 8 percent in 1949.

I do not wish to deny the critical importance of research. In absolute numbers, perhaps we as a nation need some 135,000 research scientists in the field of medicine. The testimony of experts should be thoroughly heard and scrutinized before we take a stand against supporting that number of researchers. The more apparent and immediate crisis, it seems to me, is the accompanying sharp decline in the combined supply of general practitioners and medical specialists from 61 percent in 1949 to 37 percent in 1980. The University of Pennsylvania has a long and distinguished history as a research center in the field of medicine. Surely, it is not in the national interest for institutions in that tradition to shift their focus to provide practicing doctors for the daily health needs of non-Park Avenue America.

It is very much in the national interest, however, for the leading universities to appreciate and deeply respect the total context. Great research institutions have always supplied the greatest number of teaching faculties for the network of colleges and universities across the country. Is it any wonder that the primary motivation of such faculty was to multiply and fill the earth with replications of their quality education? To be a success in a chosen profession, one might start in a lesser institution, but the aim was to bring it up to a higher standard or to use it as a stepping stone (or, better, a springboard) for a "quality" post in a quality institution. The medical profession remained unconcerned about, and even skeptical of, the development of health care delivery systems even as their own expanded professional schools sought out and educated students who would further increase the supply of non-practitioners.

The medical trend reflects the dilemmas that confront everyone in higher education. Undeniably, the broad-based population has come to higher education; the whole people have at least tentatively staked a claim to its expertise. There are educators who rejoice at this development, long having believed that educational and financial riches would soon become available to a wide range of people. But faculty who have not shared that view regard institutions with less research potential simply as social security for faculty positions. The dangers of this attitude are obvious. The young Ph.D. in renaissance literature, recognizing the dearth of faculty openings, applies to a community college in a small midwestern town as well as to Hunter College to teach reading remediation "if that's all there is." No matter which position such a faculty member obtains, students are not likely to receive quality instruction.

Teachers who are learner-centered must care about students, not in any demeaning patriarchal way but with a real respect for where they come from, who they are, and where they might be going. Only if faculties can come to respect the dignity of relating their expertise to a broad base of people with both personal and societally determined needs will we have learner-centered reform.

Major curriculum changes are empty unless the professors who teach innovative courses respond with zest and enthusiasm to the possibilities of enriching their students. Faculty members bring themselves and their intellectual formation to the enterprise. If indeed they have been liberally educated, their spirit of inquiry and their broad-based humanistic concerns will rise to the challenge. Reform will begin in individual courses and the instructors will form a new kind of collegium, challenging and reinforcing one another in a new quest to find the true relatedness of knowledge, of insight, of common endeavor.

Financial exigency forces even intellectuals to reassess their private worlds. Perhaps the almost cynical resignation of new Ph.D.s to teach the "lesser people" in an unbelievably tight labor market will bring our leadership institutions to a new humility. Perhaps they will realize that success and quality must be distributive if the family of man is to be a family of dignity. Those who are professionally as well as personally committed to the life of the mind cannot afford to support a hierarchical cult that respects only the intellect of the few. Leaders and leadership institutions will lead only if they understand that they are contingent parts within the whole.

One of the dominant symbols of Christianity is the *mystical body*: "they [are] many members, yet but one body. And the eye cannot say unto the hand, I have no need of thee: nor again the head to the feet, I have no need of you. Nay, much more these members of the body, which seem to be more feeble, are necessary." The world community and the community of higher education need to meditate on the secular but spiritual meaning of that symbol. It is obviously not a hierarchical one. It describes a body, the parts of which are *different* from one another, but *not higher* than one another.

I have tried to point to a need for distributive rather than hierarchical educational quality if we are to shape a world of equitable justice. There has been a basic philosophy deeply entrenched in the traditions of both higher education and the country. Horatio Alger might always strive to become president of the United States or a research professor at the Massachusetts Institute of Technology. That was the American Dream. But if the 1975 Horatio Alger can envision success only at the top, 90 percent of his brothers and sisters must be consigned to relative failure. If colleges and universities recruit, nurture, and send forth persons who see success for themselves and for their students only if they are at the top, they begin and nurture the self-fulfilling prophecy of mass failure; their indifference to the potential of the broad-based population means they are not doing their jobs as educators.

Learner-centered reform is contingent on teacher-centered reform. If the nation understands the reciprocal contingency—the interdependency of the expert and the laymen—there is hope that we will "re-form" each other.

4

Reform and Red Tape

Morris T. Keeton

Red tape is strangling reform in higher education. It unavoidably does. The question is not whether bureaucracy will interfere with reform, but whether the level of interference can be held to a socially useful level. By *reform*, I mean changes that will likely have a pervasive effect within their institutions and that promise substantial improvement of education. By *red tape*, I mean the costs, time, procedures and counterreformative standards that are normal to administration but are deliberately or inadvertently used to maintain the *status quo*.

Not all adverse conditions limit reform. Some even encourage it. Significant reforms have been made by institutions simply in order to survive. One such example is Antioch College, which was bankrupt in 1919 when its trustees turned it over to Arthur Morgan for whatever reform he thought might work.

Reform might also be encouraged by conditions of prosperity; it can be discarded without crisis if it fails to work. Thus, when federal and state governments provide full funding for an innovation or guarantee financing, reforms of a sweeping nature can be safely undertaken. The land-grant colleges are an example of this kind of reform. The recent federal support for expansion of equal opportunity through supplemental financial aid seemed to be such a guarantee. Unfortunately, however, the government failed to supply the continuing support implied in its initial commitments.

What I wish to discuss is neither reform out of bankruptcy nor reform with sure guarantees. It seems to me that the most genuine reform is likely to emerge from clear thinking about the causes and cures of the ills of higher education and about the sources from which major improvement might come. Interferences with this kind of reform can be extremely serious.

Oddly enough, the outright opponents of reform are not, in my view, a major threat. Their criticism tends to weed out sound from unsound reforms and to force refinement. Along with regulatory agencies, the real enemies of higher education reform are the competitors who stand to lose markets, and the supporters (or at least noncontenders) who see no need to change the procedures and standards by which reforms are legitimized. Reform requires, first of all, the opportunity to be tested with a minimum of unnecessary handicaps, and then the opportunity to be judged by standards appropriate to the perspective from which the reform is undertaken.

The current recession in higher education is accompanied, and in part accentuated, by limited opportunities to initiate new programs and institutions. Increasingly, states are adding to the procedures and regulations constraining innovation. Separate authorizations may be required for the right to do business in a state, to get program approval, to offer degrees, to be eligible for state aid to students (with veterans as a special category, and often under different terms for different aid programs), and to confer particular forms of certification (with a separate authorization for each form of certificate). Generally, the authorization to do business is a very simple matter. Often the opportunity to offer courses or programs, even for credit, is not difficult for regionally accredited institutions within the region of their headquarters, but nonaccredited institutions meet a different problem. Accredited institutions outside of their home regions may encounter delays and complications. In many cases, the sheer number of approval processes, the length of time required to go through them, the amount and level of staff investment required to make the case, and the costs of all of these matters are sufficient to discourage reformers or their sponsoring institutions from pursuing an out-of-state venture in reform. Private colleges typically face greater difficulties than public ones.

Once an institution has committed itself to seek authorization for a new program or a subordinate institution in another state, it encounters regulations (usually from a state board of higher education, a state department of education, the regents of a state higher education system, or a state coordinating board) about the conditions under which such new programs may be created. These regulations usually read like consumer protection legislation, insisting on program quality and the integrity and reliability of the institution in fulfilling its promises. Sometimes these regulations, in stipulating that "duplication" must be avoided, discourage fair competition. One quickly encounters the realities of protectionism. For example, if the reforming institution is public or large or has a long history, its chances of being considered favorably, especially within its own state, are much enhanced. Usually a very large or public institution, especially one that has already been authorized to do doctoral work, has been authorized previously in areas that can be interpreted to cover the new things it wants to do; thus, its approval can be arranged quietly and relatively quickly as a matter of administrative interpretation. The lot of "outsiders" is not so easy.

Antioch College encountered authorization problems. It had been operating four programs in a particular state with program approval as a foreign corporation. Charter was denied partly on the grounds that the already chartered institutions were under-enrolled. The denial apparently did not take into account evidence that the enrollment vacancies were for different types of programs and services. It did not mention that the Antioch programs could not possibly accommodate all applicants, the balance of whom might have been recruited by the chartered institutions had those institutions chosen to offer the innovative programs in question. Informally, some sources assured me that the charter was denied primarily because chartered institutions in that state wanted to avoid competition with the likes of Antioch. Parties who potentially could be affected by the decision (competing private colleges, a competing state system of institutions, and competing public institutions) effectively limited Antioch's opportunity to initiate and operate programs. Informally, a person associated with one of these parties advised me that he thought this situation was a violation of the Interstate Commerce Act prohibition against conspiracies in restraint of trade. But he added that even if Antioch could afford the long battle to prove the point, the regulatory agency could thereafter so constrain and harass the school so as to make it imprudent to proceed. He suggested that Antioch turn its programs over to him. It was clear that the name of a particular program might persist under his control, but not the characteristics that had made that program educationally important and successful with its students.

Typically, a new out-of-state institution or program will be approved by state authorities for only one year. By the time approval is granted, the managers of the innovation must start preparing the petition and documentation for renewal. Such requirements are not confined to state agencies. The Antioch School of Law, upon initial provisional accreditation by the American Bar Association, was required to undergo semiannual visits for ongoing approval (this requirement was soon relaxed to annual visits).

To prove in court or in legislative hearings how widespread and unfair these legalization processes are would require days and days of hearings, spaced over months or years. And preparing the evidence would require the same care as in a full-blown state examination of a proposed out-of-state program.

The primary creator of red tape is the states, but regional associations also contribute to the problem. Regulations governing the conditions under which new programs or institutions are examined do more to constrain the opportunity to initiate than anything else. The federal government, by requiring that the Institutional Eligibility Office of the U.S. Office of Education declare that an institution and its students are eligible for federal aid, actually has helped a little. Unfortunately, the authority is rarely exercised; it appears it was not primarily meant to foster reform.

Fundamental reform strikes directly or indirectly at previous conceptions of what was good or acceptable. In most regulatory agencies, the rules are designed to prevent activities that are not deemed good or acceptable under prevailing conceptions. We are moving increasingly today toward the management of higher education by public authorities. Likewise, the same authorities are coming to control their competitors—private institutions. In short, we are moving toward a monopoly of standards by public authority.

Two years ago I prepared a paper on the "hidden agendas of institutional evaluators" for the North Central Association of Colleges and Secondary Schools. In the paper I sketched a number of standards that examiners typically bring to bear, sometimes unconsciously, in judging the accreditability of the colleges they are evaluating. According to North Central policy, an institution—assuming that it qualifies as being appropriate for membership in the Association—is to be judged by its own purpose and philosophy, not by that of some other type of institution, sponsor, or school of pedagogical, religious, or ideological outlook. Yet one finds examiners judging a community college as if it were aiming to be the first half of a four-year predoctoral training school; judging an experimental university trying out purely interdisciplinary programs that stress ecological perspectives as if it were competing with a research-oriented university organized by disciplines; imposing on a Calvinistic college, where the ultimate justification is its service to God, the criterion that students and faculty should be committed to higher learning purely for learning's sake; determining that one conception of liberal arts should apply to a college whose philosophy suggests a different conception of liberal education; and even measuring very minute aspects of a university's resources and life as if what is good in Cambridge or Berkeley is ideal for all.

One of the most wrongheaded and disheartening intrusions by regulatory agencies is their equation of authoritarian administration with quality control. During the past five years, I have been asked dozens of times how I, as a provost, guarantee that program directors will comply with my orders to assure quality in college operations. The fact is, I believe that provosts who get results by authoritarian measures are engaged in a counterproductive pattern of academic administration. In higher education, of all places, there should be faith in the power of ideas and persuasion and conviction to induce outstanding performance. Yet in state, regional, and professional accrediting bodies, administrators must prove their ability to assure future quality by showing that they are martinets.

This mind-set about what is good in educational administration also results in other dysfunctional standards. For example, tradition holds that faculties should not be overworked by having to perform tasks that get in the way of good scholarship and good teaching. Thus, when examiners find instructors knocking themselves out, they may wrongly infer that an overbearing dean is making them do it. It does not occur to the examiners that in some cases faculty members might work inordinately hard because they believe passionately in the importance of what they are doing. The same applies, of course, to students.

The most readily perceived instruments for strangling reform are time and cost. The two are interrelated. In a growing number of states, an institution must possess accumulated assets that serve as a guarantee that it will not fall down on its obligations to students and to creditors. The purpose of the requirement is worthy. The method is an enormous constraint. I know of one institution, now closed, that had every prospect of becoming a high quality institution and fulfilling a significant function. Its opening was delayed for over three years while it raised and spent money trying to accumulate the $500,000 required as a guarantee. The costs of both raising the money and trying to get state approval were enormous. If the institution had opened as soon as its plans and its personnel were in good array, its operating income would have enabled it to accumulate the guarantee or at the very least to meet its obligations to its students if it failed to continue. A possible solution to such problems would be a state or federally established guarantee pool available to innovating institutions that can provide evidence of good planning and a competent staff.

Also contributing to time-and-cost strangulation is the petitioning process institutions must go through to obtain authorization to grant accredited degrees. As I have already mentioned, such processes are not a matter of one petition to one authority; the number of submissions required differs depending on the state, region, and type of degree. Normally, the petitions required for a state body differ from those required for regional accrediting, and both of these petitions differ from those required for professional accreditation, such as in law, medicine, and social work. An established institution with several thousand students and an annual budget of over 10 million dollars can afford to spend $100,000 a year for several years to develop and sustain its credentials. This represents only one percent of its resources. But a struggling new endeavor might find itself devoting 20 percent or more of its resources to trying to obtain credentials. And this percentage is enough to undermine the institution's quality or to drive it out of the market.

The use of political power to encourage or suppress reform is one of the more distressing aspects of the relationship between reform and regulation. Unless government agencies, voluntary associations, and educational institutions and their personnel develop an ethic that supports pluralism of purpose, philosophy, and methodology in higher education, and act accordingly, reforms in the mechanics of regulation will not provide the needed change. I am not making a naive plea for an end to politics, but I am saying that a new kind of politics is needed in order to achieve a lasting and satisfactory solution to the difficulties of higher education reform. In this new politics, professional interests will be outweighed by consumer interests, and institutional self-serving will be met with counterweights from public interests and competing institutional interests.

Will the red tape associated with these efforts grow to such lengths that new reforms are choked off at birth? I wonder.

5

Role of Statewide Boards in Program Review

Elizabeth H. Johnson

Statewide coordinating and planning boards or commissions were almost invisible only a few years ago. The closest example in a few states, including Oregon, were single state-level governing or policy-making boards for all of the publicly supported colleges and universities. At first, statewide coordinating councils were formed to assist in the voluntary coordination of institutions with respect to federal funding provisions. Then, as these voluntary entities became regulatory, and as their role became more threatening to the long-accepted autonomy of traditional institutions, state legislatures often made them statewide governing boards or strengthened their regulatory powers. Under the federal Higher Education Amendments of 1972, many of these state-level boards have now been named the "1202 Commissions" for state-wide planning. They are the "new kid on the block." Their proper roles are evolving, and they are being eyed with some suspicion and criticism even though the need for some kind of coordination and rational planning is now generally accepted.

John Folger, Executive Director, Tennessee Education Commission, asked some basic questions that must be considered when we talk about the rapid development of statewide boards:

First, how much planning? Or, to what extent should we utilize planning and to what extent should we rely on competition and market forces to determine the future development of post-secondary education?

Second, who should do it? Or, what is the political context within which planning should occur?

Third, how should it be done? Or, do we have an adequate technology of planning?[1]

There are many converging forces creating a situation in every state for political and education leaders to reexamine the structural and the delegated powers of their existing boards and commissions. Leaders must also look at the capability of the boards to carry out their duties and responsibilities not in the interests of what is good for the internal constituencies of education—the faculties, administrators, students and trustees—but what best serves the illusive, but all-important "public" interests and justifies the vast expenditures of public and private funds, and tuition.

Structures for governing and coordinating higher education are changing. One example is the action on the part of the governor of Maine, James B. Longley, who asked for the resignation of all members of the University of Maine board, believing this would make the university more accountable to taxpayers and students. The proposed dissolution of the Ohio board of regents by Governor James Rhodes, who created the regents originally, is another. I think it is safe to say that in almost every state that has not recently changed its governing or coordinating structure, the traditional organizations are in trouble.

[1]John K. Folger, "Three Questions about Statewide Planning," in John F. Hughes and Olive Mills, eds., *Formulating Policy in Postsecondary Education: A Search for Alternatives* (Washington, D.C.: American Council on Education, 1975), pp. 227-228.

Just rearranging the tables of organization or abolishing one structure and creating another will not solve coordination problems. The fact that the political leaders have been taking the initiative and leadership role, though, is significant. Education leaders must do more than criticize and raise the rallying cry of "academic freedom" and "institutional autonomy" and get the wagons in a ring to protect the status quo. If we believe in the necessity of continuous planning, both short- and long-range; if we believe in diversity of options for students and for society; if we believe in accountability for the use of available funds, then we have to recognize that a plan, like a budget, is a mechanism of control. An individual institution is restricted in its "autonomy" or its authorization to go its own way by that control mechanism. Since control is the reality, it may be impossible to avoid tension and conflict between the planners and the educational establishment. I join those who believe that any governing scheme depends on the willingness of persons of good will and broad understanding to stand back and see what it is that must be accomplished. If the planning is done cooperatively, and if the planners are not trying to "govern" at the same time as they try to administer and operate, then confrontation is avoidable.

Since the primary responsibility for education rests with the state, the final decision may have to be a political one in the end. Congress and the state legislatures hold the purse strings. Personalities are bound to be a strong influence, but the wise administrator, planner, and leader will all recognize the realities. It is crucial that the people who pay for the education (kindergarten through graduate school), the employers, the practitioners, and the consumers be an important part of the planning process.

D. Kent Halstead takes a look at control in the form of a centralized coordinating and planning board, and says:

The debate regarding centralized versus decentralized authority in higher education has progressed beyond arguing the relative advantages and disadvantages of each. Discussion of the pros and cons of both central coordination and institutional autonomy has resulted in considerable agreement among educators about the relative merits of both practices. The evidence also reveals—and herein lies the crux of the controversy—that a winning combination is a yet unidentified balance which would retain most of the advantages of central control with a minimal sacrifice of institu-

tional sovereignty. . . . The balance sought is delicate, and equilibrium may exist only in theory.

No effective planning agency can expect to fulfill all the hopes and aspirations of each institution. No institution is likely to endorse all the coordination measures proposed by a state-level agency. Consequently, it is realistic to expect that some form of power struggle will always be inevitable—maybe a healthy sign. . . . It is likely that no two states will weigh the values of autonomy and coordination in exactly the same manner.[2]

Even given many dissimilarities, how much power or authority should the planning and coordinating agency have? Here I turn to the best minds in the research and development field, my own experience, and the trends in the separate states and at the federal level. By every indicator, I am pursuaded that the coordinating agency, which occupies a kind of middle ground between the institutions and the political decision-makers, should have at least the five minimum powers named by Lyman A. Glenny and others and those listed in the report of the Education Commission of the States, "Coordination or Chaos": "to engage in continuous planning, both long-range and short-range; to acquire information from all postsecondary institutions and agencies through the establishment of statewide management and data systems; to review and approve new and existing programs, new campuses, extension centers, departments and centers of all public institutions, and, where substantial state aid is given, of all private institutions; to review and make recommendations on any and all facets of both operating and capital budgets, and when requested by state authorities, present a consolidated budget for the whole system; and to administer directly, or have under its coordinative powers all state scholarship and grant programs to students, grant programs to nonpublic institutions and all state-administered federal grant and aid programs."[3]

Many oppose granting any of these powers to a coordinating board; others might oppose certain ones; but my reading of the

[2]D. Kent Halstead, *Statewide Planning in Higher Education* (Washington, D.C.: Government Printing Office, 1974).

[3]Lyman A. Glenny, Robert O. Berdahl, Ernest G. Palola, and James G. Paltridge, *Coordinating Higher Education for the 70's.* Report for the Center for Research and Development in Higher Education, University of California, Berkeley, 1971.

current scene, state by state, indicates that program review and budget review are the most important and sensitive areas. There is no one "best" arrangement or delineation of powers because no two states have the same demographic patterns, traditions, and existing structures. The policy-makers in the various state governments, however, have similar needs. They need to know that continuous planning is going on, and that budget requests are linked to realistic goals of both institutions and state government. They need to know that the public interest has been represented in the planning, along with institutional and student interests. They need balanced, comparable, unbiased, analyzed data on which to base the policy decisions that they must make in appropriating funds.

Actually, it is often true that if clear and considerable powers are granted, they will not need to be used. Time that otherwise might be spent arguing about jurisdiction or authority questions could be spent more constructively. If the rights and responsibilities of all the actors are known, voluntary cooperation often follows more easily or forthrightly. The conclusions reached by many experts in the field are stated clearly by Glenny: "The choice today is not between strengthening the coordinating board or retaining the status quo. Rather, the choice is between creating an effective coordinating board or of seeing postsecondary education ingested into the executive branch of state government. [I would add "or, under control of the legislative branch."] Strengthened coordination seems the best way to protect the public interest in education with minimum impairment of institutional autonomy. . . . Whatever the number and variety of substructures subject to coordinating board jurisdiction, the board and its staff should exercise power over institutions only through the official channels of the particular institution or subsystem."[4]

There are two key jurisdictional issues between the coordinating board and the institutional or segmental policy (governing) boards: Where should the line be drawn between their respective powers and responsibilities, and how can it be made clear that there are areas of institutional or system-wide governance that the coordinating board should not be involved in? These are sensitive matters. As one person has aptly put it: "The idea that 'outsiders,' state bureaucrats or representatives of a political environment

[4]Glenny and others.

might meddle in academic affairs probably transcends all of the other administrative and coordinative issues relating to statewide coordination of postsecondary education."[5]

Despite the legitimate and traditional reservations about the roles of statewide coordinating boards, the number and power of these boards have increased in recent years. Section 1202 of the Higher Education Amendments of 1972 has prompted both the creation of new planning or coordinating agencies and the renaming of existing agencies as 1202 Commissions. Increasingly, too, the function of program review and approval has become commonplace, but it is still in the beginning stages of the art.

A survey by the Education Commission of the States shows that of the forty-five states having coordinating agencies with statutory authority to review and approve or recommend programs, thirty-seven have the responsibility to review and approve programs. Eight statewide coordinating agencies, including the Oregon Educational Coordinating Council, have statutory responsibility to review and recommend only. In five states, the responsibility to review and recommend is a matter of policy, not of statute. As the role of these agencies has evolved from "voluntary" to "advisory" responsibilities, to regulatory powers, and in a few more recent cases, to governing authorities, the function of program review has become commonplace.

By the broad term *program*, I refer to those organized educational activities, excluding individual courses and course content, which lead to some terminal objective: a degree, diploma, certificate, or license. Under the umbrella of program, I include departments, divisions, schools, colleges, institutes, learning centers, branches, or any unit not presently included in the program of the institution. It usually does not include "reasonable and moderate" extensions of existing curricula, research or public service programs, except where they may overlap and compete unreasonably with those of nearby institutions—both public and private.

Broadly stated, the purposes of program review are to conserve resources, to avoid unnecessary and unwise duplication and proliferation, to assure quality programs, and to assess the state's

[5] Robert J. Barak, "Survey of State-Level Academic Program Review Policies and Procedures for Higher Education." Paper prepared for the State Higher Education Executive Officers, February 19, 1975.

needs for a given program. In the case of high-cost specialized professional programs, such as veterinary medicine, health professions, and oceanography, there must be regional planning and needs assessment to increase access to high-quality programs and conserve resources Consortia and regional efforts are underway, and they too must be encouraged.

Apparently many states have concluded "that neither the organs of state government nor the institutions of higher education are capable of conducting finely balanced assessments involved in program review—the government agencies because the issues are too complex for nonprofessionals to handle, and the institutions because their own self-interest often inhibits their objectivity."[6] To expect an institution to act as its own physician, diagnosing the weak programs, especially in times of financial stress, and then getting out the instruments and performing surgery where indicated, is asking too much. Thus, the functions fall on nonadministrative coordinating agencies.

Where financial exigencies have required an institution to reduce or eliminate programs, the process and the results have been traumatic for both the institution and the public. The press, under the stipulation of "open meeting" laws, frequently has demanded the right to attend and report deliberations that affect the people linked with the programs being considered. In some cases, the announced program reductions have been more publicized than real. In others, even a small improvement in either the financial or enrollment situation of the institution has dampened enthusiasm for program reduction. Most institutions, although they may agree on the principle of state-level review and recommendation, would dissent from the specific processes and choose voluntary compliance—or, if forced, across-the-board reductions—rather than the termination or shelving of programs.

In any event, if a goal of program reduction is to conserve resources, terminating a program will not, in and of itself, reduce expenditure outlays unless faculty is reduced. If a degree is dropped, but the courses and the instructors to teach them are retained and shifted into other programs, no money is saved. If the degree is no longer offered, but the courses remain, enrollment

---

[6]Robert O. Berdahl, *Statewide Coordination of Higher Education* (Washington, D.C.: American Council on Education, 1971).

may decline in those courses, thus increasing the unit costs. If the courses and the degree are eliminated, but the tenured faculty who taught them are transferred to other teaching or administrative posts, no sizeable savings result. If a program is retained with the recommendation of improving quality, costs are increased. As Glenny puts it: "Whatever the economics of steady state and the politics of tenure, the analyses of program elimination must consider a reduction in faculty—or no great savings in dollars will result."[7]

The words *master plan* raise all kinds of questions and mistrust. And the warning that a master plan must not become *the* master plan, cast in concrete, is a valid one. However, before any statewide governing or coordinating board can consider change or program review, it has to ask searching and perhaps uncomfortable questions about the current state of planning. Whether we like it or not, there has to be some kind of overall plan, some thoroughly considered statement of educational goals for the state, the system, the individual institutions, and the programs themselves. Policy boards at the institutional level are obliged to assure that their institutions have valid, objective, studied master plans that are continually brought up to date.

Too often, statements of guidelines or goals have been cast in such "global" and idealistic terms that they are relatively meaningless—or they have been stated in the kind of educational jargon that makes them less than clear, even to the educators. Obfuscating language just asks the lay citizen to be skeptical, if not disbelieving. Without getting caught up in the details of how a broadbased planning group ought to organize itself, let me simply suggest the kinds of questions that I believe ought to be raised: Does the state have a master plan that includes statements of the missions of all institutions, public, private, and proprietary? Are these missions realistically laid out so they can serve as guidelines for planning and evaluation? Does the master plan define the roles and responsibilities of the existing governing or coordinating boards and individual institutional boards? Is there an up-to-date inventory of all the programs presently available and where they

[7]Lyman A. Glenny, *Institutional Response to the Steady State* (Berkeley: Center for Research and Development in Higher Education, University of California, Berkeley, 1975).

are? Has a study been made of unmet needs? What is the current statutory or policy provision for reviewing and approving programs? By what agencies? Which programs are to be reviewed? What kind of provision for planning and coordination would best serve the state, with its own traditions, its existing structures for governance and policy-making, and its unique political climate?

If, based on its findings, the statewide planning group recommends a strong state-level agency to resolve issues that individual institutions or system-wide or segmental policy boards and state governments cannot resolve, then program review and recommendation and the effectiveness of education programs at all levels become top priority items of the coordinating body. A nonadministering board can raise the kind of questions and call for the kind of planning, decision making, and management that will produce change, promote cooperative efforts, and anticipate issues and problems.

Coordinating boards must develop their own guidelines and operating procedures, again fitted to the situation in each state. In evaluating what is being done, what ought or might be done, and what outcomes may be expected, specific and clear goals statements for the state, for the segments, and for the institutions are vital. In 1947, President Truman's Commission on Higher Education offered this advice: "What America needs today is a schooling better aware of its aims. Our colleges need to see clearly what it is they are trying to accomplish and they need ways of measuring their effectiveness in meeting those aims."[8] That advice is even more relevant today. With more than 50 percent of the college-age group going on to postsecondary education of some kind, the education missions of an institution must be clear, visible, and understood by students, the public, and by the elected and appointed persons responsible for the effective and efficient operation of the schools.

In reviewing programs, proposed and existing, the state-level board will have to concern itself with three broad aspects, as identified and described by Glenny and associates: the programs to be reviewed, the criteria to be used in judging, and the mechanism of review.[9] Obviously, the programs to be reviewed will depend on

[8] Virginia B. Smith, "Assessment and Educational Policy," *Planning for Higher Education*, 1975, 4(1), 1.
[9] Glenny and others.

the legal authority of the coordinating or governing board. The case has been made, I believe, that the most effective process of review is one that considers not only the approval of new programs, but also the deletion, merger, reallocation, and suspension of existing programs.

The membership of the board should be made up of knowledgeable, experienced *lay* persons not connected directly with, or employed by, public institutions or agencies. They need time, interest, and energy to devote to the task. They should assure themselves that they have a competent director or commissioner and a staff experienced in the areas of board responsibility. The staff may be relatively small if it utilizes the planning and information gathering capabilities of the institutional and segmental levels. With the aid of the staff, the statewide board should establish the criteria for program review. In general, these criteria should call for the use of common guidelines and procedures.

In relation to the central issue in program review—that of the mechanism and the process of review—I want to avoid details and alternate processes because they are almost limitless. Generally, the mechanism or process of review needs to be responsive to the following conditions: It must take into consideration the jurisdiction and powers of existing boards, systems, and substructures. It should utilize common guidelines and procedures so that all institutions are responding to the same requests and requirements. It should involve the individual institutions and their faculties, administrators, and students in developing the plans and guidelines. It should contain no unnecessary and cumbersome features. It should expedite change, if recommended. It should require statewide compliance with the process. It should allow decisions about individual courses and course content to stay at the institutional level. It should deal with the matter of de facto programs that operate without formal approval. It should provide for standing and ad hoc advisory committees that may or may not include coordinating board members, but that may utilize coordinating board staff assistance. It should provide for the use of outside consultants, for on-site visits by consultants from inside and outside the state. It should work closely with the institutional and segmental boards and staffs in developing recommendations. Finally, individual institutions or the segments should be required to respond to questions concerning their goals, their educational relevancy, and their cost efficiency.

The history of higher education indicates that much of the impetus for change and diversity has come from student demand and from the outside, particularly from the political world. Some of the responses have been outstandingly good. We have moved from higher education for relatively few to mass postsecondary education attracting more and more new learners. In the process, however, we may be lowering standards and accepting mediocre performance that debases the worth of the credentials. It is imperative that state-level boards provide leadership in assessing the performance, in forecasting "futures," and in providing opportunities to examine economic, social, and demographic forces, issues, and trends as these apply to education in the state. Such a coordinating board would be responsible, then, for acting as a bridge between institutions and the decision-makers in state government. Because of the rapid growth of postsecondary education in the past two decades, and the lack of time for careful planning, many inequalities have developed. We have to answer simple but difficult questions: Who should pay? For what? Where? How much? For how long?

Also, it will be increasingly necessary for all boards to assess periodically, and even harshly, their own performances in the light of their changing roles. Because the planning, information gathering, coordinative, and evaluative functions of state-level boards are different from those of policy-making boards (and they are relative latecomers), state boards will have to be especially diligent in performing and assessing those functions. James Miller put it this way: "Some agencies have more power than their enabling legislation suggests because they are heavy on informal power, influence, and 'credibility' with state officials and the public. Other agencies have less power than the statutes suggest because their credibility is low and their recommendations are ignored. The web of informal relationships, communication, and respect among legislators and the state agency is extremely important and is often overlooked."[10]

The situation in New York State, described by Karen Winkler,[11] points to the gap that exists between theory and the actual

[10]James L. Miller, Jr. as quoted by Robert O. Berdahl in a paper presented to IEP, San Francisco, February 1975.
[11]Karen Winkler, "Statewide Planning Versus Institutional Autonomy," *Chronicle of Higher Education,* January 27, 1975.

"review and approve" process. The commissioners of education and the regents, who are appointed by the legislature and must "register" (approve) all programs in both public and private colleges and universities, have undertaken to review and recommend continuance, termination, phase out, or improvement of all doctoral programs in the state. Their recommendations have been intensely questioned by the chancellor and regents of the state university system and by individual presidents.

Everyone admits that the two criteria used—need and quality—are difficult to come to grips with. It has been customary to link quality with dollars expended, faculty degree and salary levels, space utilized, library holdings, and the like. If there are studies that show direct relationships between dollars and effectiveness of outcomes, I don't know of any—although there are obvious relationships between resources available and choices that may then be made. The use of need as an evaluative criterion—whether in reference to the needs of society for trained manpower, or the needs of students—runs counter to the long-held tradition that students ought to be able to enroll in any program they wish and for which they are qualified, whether or not there will be an employment outlet for their training and talents. This as well as other certain well established status requirements have led institutions to try to offer a vast smorgasbord of studies. Rapidly increasing enrollments have justified most programs, even in fields that are not very popular. Duplication of most undergraduate programs and departmental majors at state colleges and universities has been the rule. The federal government has poured money into a variety of programs, thus compounding the proliferation.

At these crossroads in the long history of the development and financing of higher education, it may be to the advantage of the state and the institution to consolidate programs for which there is decreased demand or disproportionate costs. The powers of program termination or reallocation have been used but slightly up to now. Ralph Dungan, chancellor of higher education in New Jersey, is quoted in a recent *Chronicle of Higher Education* article as saying that some institutions have developed "a Brinks-truck mentality: you dump the dough once a year and you don't come back and see us again until next year."[12] This article raises the

---

[12]Philip W. Semas, "Push Meets Shove in Jersey," *Chronicle of Higher Education*, December 16, 1974.

question of what will happen when a strong state coordinating agency comes up against a strong statewide faculty union.

College presidents are predictably upset by the prospects, as are faculties. They see the whole process of state-level program review and recommendation as infringing on their traditional autonomy and responsibility. Though some of them publicly denounce the specifics of the review process while endorsing the general principles, privately they will admit that the state-level reviews may give them more latitude and power to eliminate weak programs that sap their funds. The review process could improve image, credibility, and drawing power of the institution. Given adequate information and counseling, students will choose strong programs.

Glenny in "The Volatile Steady State" says: "At the state level, concern must be focused toward flexibility, zero-base planning, clearly defined, realistic goals and objectives for each institution, adherence to long-range plans through such goals and an operationally responsive planning and budgeting process."[13] In my view, these are proper concerns for a state-level agency. The executive director of the agency should be able to stimulate his board members and educate them objectively and persistently about present and future issues. If there are academic deficits, he should encourage planning to alleviate them.

Somebody has to do it. Internally, the faculties find it extremely difficult to reach these kinds of decisions. They lack the statewide perspective, and their self-interests blur vision. Externally, it is more appropriate that program review and approval be done by a statewide coordinating board that includes all levels of education than by a governor's staff or a legislative staff. Most legislators do not want to serve as education board members, and they resent being cast in the role of academic "meddlers," or accused of being niggardly if they do not fund budget requests at a level near the asking.

Some observers would advise against creating or strengthening coordinating boards and ask, "Is this not an invasion of academic freedom?" The reply is that nothing recommended here would preclude an institution from engaging in self-evaluation and priority setting. In fact, the processes accompanying coordinating review boards would encourage faculties and administrators to

[13]Lyman A. Glenny, "The Volatile Steady State." Mimeographed speech. Berkeley: Center for Research and Development in Higher Education, University of California, August 30, 1974.

find ways to improve their offerings, management, and operations. If institutions choose to buck the current trends and fight the legislatures or the statewide coordinating boards, they will lose. On the other hand, if they choose to join the effort, they will have taken an important step forward in regaining public confidence and support.

PART TWO

State of the Art

One of the dominant ideas behind educational reforms of the fif-
ties and sixties was "education for all." In the opening chapter of
Part Two, K. Patricia Cross, whose writings have influenced a number of reforms in higher education, gives a slight but significant
twist to the idea by proposing that the mandate for the seventies
should be "education for each." Confining her remarks to curricular reform, Cross acknowledges that progress has already been
made in recognizing the different rates at which individuals learn
and the different life situations from which they come. But much
work remains to be done, she believes, in adjusting the curriculum
to fit different learning styles and different learning goals.

Research on instructional techniques has been inconclusive,
Cross points out. About the only conclusion one can draw from it
is that no single technique—lecture, discussion, independent study,
whatever—is clearly best for all students. The "average" student
may do as well under any technique, but individual students will
not. They need the chance to sample various learning styles and
choose the ones that suit them best. With goals, Cross finds the

problem to be one of unifying rhetoric, practice, and real life. This presently discordant trinity is represented by the catalogue, the classroom, and a student's personal life, respectively. Although some efforts are underway to bring the first two into accord, Cross says, little attention has been given to the third.

The remaining chapters of Part Two do not assess the state of learner-centered reform as much as they reflect it. A. Paul Bradley, Jr., describes faculty roles in contract learning, and Jack Lindquist proposes several strategies for launching contract learning at institutions. Both writers draw their material from experiences at Empire State College, but Lindquist also refers to case studies of contract learning at the University of South Carolina and Wilmington College.

In a more general way, Jerry G. Gaff also deals with the role of faculty. Gaff, director of the Center for Professional Development at California State University and Colleges, sees three major trends emerging from the many professional development programs now underway. He identifies these as instructional development, faculty development, and organizational development. Once educators recognize these three aspects of professional development, and learn to distinguish them from one another, Gaff feels that much of the confusion surrounding professional development will abate.

The two concluding chapters of this part describe programs that vividly illustrate the idea of fitting college to the learner's life situation. Sylvia G. McCollum discusses the unique problems of providing college programs for prisoners, both during and after confinement, and Victor P. Meskill describes the successful Weekend College launched by the C. W. Post Center of Long Island University in 1971. Both authors see the principle of reaching and serving new clienteles—of sending college to people—as having great potential that is relatively untapped. McCollum and Meskill are concerned less about reforming educational content and method than about devising mechanisms to make existing educational programs more accessible. The problems identified by McCollum, for example, relate mainly to time, location, facilities, and cost. Meskill also suggests that these problems will have to be met; according to him, the success of Weekend College stems from choosing appropriate traditional programs and scheduling them at a time when working adults can take part in them.

Although the authors of Part Two are optimistic about the state of learner-centered reform, they are also keenly aware of the unfinished business of nontraditional education—and that includes additional internal reforms to assure education for each and additional external reforms to assure education for all.

William Ferris

6

Learner-Centered Curricula

K. Patricia Cross

The typical American college has three curricula—what we say we teach, what we do teach, and what students learn. Thus we have a catalogue curriculum, a teaching curriculum, and a learning curriculum. The curriculum statement printed in the catalogue frequently bears only the faintest resemblance to what is taught by faculty; and what is taught by faculty may have surprisingly little relationship to what is learned by students. It is like playing a giant game of rumor; the message that is received is not always the message that was sent. The original message from the college, the catalogue statement, is usually a carefully worked out, reasonably sophisticated concept of what the curriculum committee and the goals committee want education at their institution to be. As this message is implemented by faculty, it becomes eligible for its first distortion; as it is received by students, it may be subject to further distortion.

Some faculty have high fidelity equipment in that they receive and transmit the educational message with relatively little distortion. Other faculty are using such old and antiquated equipment with so much static in the system that they may never receive the message at all. Or, if they do, they are unable to transmit it with anything resembling faithful reproduction. Still others can understand a sophisticated incoming message, but they lack the higher level skills required to transmit it to students. Then, a few exceptional teachers add personal touches that make the message stick indelibly in the minds of the recipients.

The catalogue curriculum is public knowledge, but the teaching and learning curricula are not well known. Only within the past few years have we dared even to look at the teaching curriculum. A professor's classroom is his castle, and few have had the temerity to question what goes on there. Although academic research is subject to open and penetrating criticism by colleagues, the academic code of honor still maintains that colleagues may not observe teaching unless invited to do so. Happily, faculty are beginning to invite the help of their colleagues more and more; mutual support through class observations and pedagogical discussions is an increasing trend. In addition, the new emphasis on faculty development is helping some instructors develop skills to improve the teaching curriculum.

Learning curriculum has not yet received much attention, however. To be sure, research studies describing the "hidden curriculum" show us what students have learned. We now know quite a bit about what happens to students as they proceed through college. Although it is still painfully apparent that the admissions office has more influence over the quality of the graduating class than instructional faculty have, some changes do seem to take place during college. On the average, students make significant gains in subject matter knowledge and in their ability to think critically. They also gain in personal integration and autonomy, in flexibility and open-mindedness, and in intellectual and cultural interests.[1] Further research on what happens to the average student on the average campus would probably be redundant. What we need

[1] Arthur W. Chickering, *Education and Identity* (San Francisco: Jossey-Bass, 1969).

to know if we are to make improvements is *who* changes and *why*. Some students regress, while others make almost unbelievable gains, and we know little about the conditions of learning that are responsible for either.

Almost everyone has his or her own vision of a student-centered curriculum. Some academics are turned off by the very term, equating it, I suspect, with a student-*determined* curriculum or perhaps with a *self*-centered curriculum. Neither fits my idea of a student-centered curriculum. Although it may be desirable, students need *not* determine the nature of their learning experiences in order for high quality learning to occur. I specifically reject the notion that self-indulgence and "doing your own thing" help to motivate students to acquire the hard self-discipline that learning requires. Having rejected such concepts as misunderstandings, I have to ask where the curriculum is centered if it is not centered in the students.

Let me offer my definition of a student-centered curriculum. I believe that the purpose of this curriculum is to make learning maximally effective—not for the *average* student, but for *each* student. Thus, a curriculum is student-centered to the extent that it provides for individual differences in learning. A course of study, for example, that does not provide for individual differences in learning rates is not maximally effective; it bores fast learners, frustrates slow learners, and results in negative learning experiences for both groups. *Student-centered reform in the curriculum is a question of finding ways to maximize learning for each student.* And that is not as difficult or as expensive as it sounds. In fact, we are already making substantial progress toward individualizing education.

I identify four major dimensions important to learning, and contend that students differ in relation to each one. They differ in rate of learning, in life situation, in learning style, and in goals. Two of these dimensions are receiving a great deal of attention today; the other two are just beginning to surface. We know quite a bit about reforming the learning curriculum through self-paced learning modules and about gearing education to the situational needs of such nontraditional learners as working adults, retired persons, prisoners, and others whose situations require special consideration. We do not know as much about gearing instruction to the cognitive styles of learners, nor have we done any really serious thinking about reform in the content and goals of the curriculum.

Individual differences in the rate of learning became a very obvious and serious problem for colleges when large-scale, open admissions began in the 1960s. Open-door colleges were faced with staggering diversity. It didn't take long to discover that there was simply no way to make an instructional program maximally useful to a student reading at the fifth grade level and to one reading at the fourteenth grade level without individualizing instruction.

Fortunately for higher education, advances in the psychology of learning had already paved the way for practical applications of reinforcement theory in the form of self-instructional modular units. It was now possible for students to control the rate at which new material could be assimilated. This breakthrough led to the much more sophisticated and attractive self-pacing models that exist in all kinds of colleges and universities today. Two-thirds of the community colleges—more than double the number only five short years ago—use self-paced learning modules.[2] The audio-tutorial program introduced at Purdue University a little more than 10 years ago has made a powerful impact on teaching in the natural sciences.[3] The Keller Plan or PSI, first introduced in this country in 1968, has revolutionized teaching in some disciplines within the last few years. Today, there are probably around 1000 PSI courses in psychology alone, and the rather sophisticated learning principles embodied in PSI are sweeping across other disciplines—especially physics and engineering—at a phenomenal rate.

There is no longer any doubt that self-pacing is both feasible and desirable as far as student learning is concerned. But what is good for students is not always convenient for teachers and administrators. The promise of self-instructional units has forced educators to examine their priorities. Most institutions and instructors have compromised; they permit students to pace themselves as long as they do so within the administratively convenient term or

[2]K. P. Cross, "1970 to 1975: Years of Change in Community Colleges," *Findings* (quarterly newsletter of the Educational Testing Service), May 1975, 2(2).
[3]S. N. Postlethwait, "Independent Study in Biology," in R. A. Weisgerber, ed., *Developmental Efforts in Individualized Learning* (Itasca, Ill.: F. E. Peacock, 1971).

semester. An ideal student-centered curriculum would permit students to complete learning units in accordance with their needs rather than ours. I think that day will arrive when colleges will take the logical, rather than the traditional, approach and will credit learning by units mastered rather than by time served.

The egalitarian push to make postsecondary education available to all also ushered in the second dimension of individual differences—that of life situation. The largest group of citizens systematically excluded from education by the classical model of a college was composed of those who were unable to pursue formal education full time. In 1972, the number of part-time students began to exceed the number of full-time students in institutions of higher education. Part-timers now constitute the majority of American college students, and the growth rate of part-time students in the 1970s has been more than three times that for full-time students. This means that the *majority* of students today have other responsibilities. Colleges can no longer confidently expect students to be free to arrange their lives and schedules in conformance with institutional procedures. Schedules, services, and even locations have had to become student-centered rather than institution-centered, and the massive move to offer programs and services attractive to part-time adult learners continues. The speed with which this student-centered reform has made its imprint on education is, I suspect, unrivaled in the history of higher education. Well over half of an estimated 2000 nontraditional programs in this country today were launched since 1970.

For a combination of reasons—some institution-centered and some student-centered—colleges have shown great willingness, even eagerness, to make it easy for people from all walks of life to attend college. If they can't come to us, we will take the college to them through new technologies or through off-campus locations in shopping centers, prisons, industry, and wherever an economically viable number of students can be assembled. I suspect that higher education has done more in the area of adapting to the life situations of individual students than in any other area of student-centered reform. In fact, I wish now that we could balance our eagerness for revising procedures and structures by carefully considering what it is what we are so eager to deliver to everyone. Are we offering education with a form and content that is maximally useful to students and society as we move towards the year 2000?

In relation to the third dimension, learning style, we have not made nearly as much progress. We have not cast the form and content of education in ways that are maximally useful to individuals, even though we are increasingly able to offer education at a rate, a time, and a place geared to individual needs. It now seems quite clear that we are not going to improve instruction by finding the method or methods that are good for all people. I suspect that research on teaching effectiveness has been inconclusive and disappointing because we have been asking the wrong questions. When we ask whether discussion is better than lecture, whether TV is as good as a live teacher, whether programmed instruction is an improvement over more traditional methods, we find that for the mythical statistical *average* student it seems to make little difference how we teach. But when we look at the data student by student, it is clear that some students improve, some remain unaffected, and some actually regress under various teaching conditions. The very process of averaging the pluses, the minuses, and the non-changers wipes out the message that different methods work for different students. Psychologists are now asking more sophisticated interaction questions about learning styles—which methods work for which students?

While we do not yet know enough about individual learning styles to prescribe strategies that will maximize learning for a given person, it is clear that we need to give more attention to offering pluralistic alternatives. Jerome Bruner puts it this way: "The fact of individual differences argues for pluralism and for an enlightened opportunism in the materials and methods of instruction. . . . A curriculum, in short, must contain many tracks leading to the same general goal."[4]

Community colleges, especially, have found that pluralism in educational methods is necessary to deal effectively with the diversity of student learning styles. Colleges concerned about undergraduate learning are offering lessons via pluralistic routes such as lecture, discussion groups, learning laboratories, media presentations, peer tutoring, and project learning. Pluralism in instructional strategies need not be institutionally determined, however. Some of the more sophisticated learning programs offer

---

[4]J. S. Bruner, *Toward a Theory of Instruction* (Cambridge, Mass.: Harvard University Press, 1966).

a variety of learning strategies within a single class. The audio-tutorial method, for example, includes printed materials, physical objects, projection visuals, and audio tapes, as well as lectures and small discussion seminars.

Variety also can be introduced into the curriculum by increasing the opportunities for experiential learning, which is popular precisely because it provides enormous variety in both resources and methods. Learning through modeling, object manipulation, and problem-solving not only offers more options than the overly restrictive paper-and-pencil learning, but it is more reality-oriented and more relevant to the lifelong learning that is required of anyone living in a rapidly changing society.

Although it will be nice when research is able to tell us more about cognitive styles, student-centered reform of the curriculum does not hinge upon our ability to prescribe specific learning strategies for each student. When options and variety are offered, students may sample all forms of presentation, consciously or subconsciously learning more through one mode than another. Or, made aware of cognitive styles, students may diagnose their own learning patterns and choose the presentations that seem useful and effective for them.

Let's now consider the fourth major dimension of the student-centered curriculum—the goals of learning. A learner-centered curriculum does not mean that individual learners must necessarily determine their own goals, although the learning contract has undeniable advantages. But such a curriculum does recognize that the goals of learning are necessarily individualistic. I suspect we would agree that it is not as important for all students to pass a standardized comprehensive subject matter examination as it is for them to make appropriate judgments and contributions on the basis of their education. We may have a beautiful set of catalogue goals, professors may be quite dedicated to the fullest possible intellectual development for students; but in the final analysis goals must be reflected in the learning curriculum if they are to have a real impact on students.

I suggest that we launch a truth-in-advertising campaign for education—one that tries to aim our teaching practices toward our catalogue goals. A good catalogue statement of goals is a joy to behold, and the hearts of educators beat with pride when they read, "The university endeavors, through the tools of learning, to develop breadth of mind, tolerance of spirit, and strength of character" or "The educational effort . . . is directed toward leading the student to be an independent seeker in his own right, not a passive recipient of information, and to assume responsibility for gaining both knowledge and judgment that will enhance his later contribution to society."

While we may hope for such admirable results, we do precious little to see that they occur. Most faculty adopt a somewhat narrower set of goals than those in the catalogue. Faculty subscribe to goals such as cultivating the intellectual skills of problem-solving, synthesis, and analysis as the appropriate teaching curriculum. When it gets to implementation, however, a substantial number merely demonstrate the accumulation of information in their academic disciplines. By the time we get around to assessing the learning curriculum, we face the tragic reality that we have not turned out students who even grasp the significance of the catalogue statements of educational goals, let alone incorporate them into their lives.

One of the most difficult, but most important, of all educational goals is the ability to make sound value judgments. As we watched the parade of highly educated Watergate participants reveal their value priorities, we knew unquestionably that it was a commentary on our failure to achieve this goal. American educators have been extremely cautious about venturing into the area of personal values, lest value education turn into indoctrination. Yet we want our students to be able to make the value judgments that doctors, lawyers, businessmen, legislators, teachers, scientists, and all educated persons are perpetually called upon to make in their professional as well as in their personal lives. It is fair to say, I think, that few educators face the value issue squarely and ask what can be done about it.

One professor who has asked that question, Lawrence Kohlberg, now teaches a popular freshman course in moral development at Harvard. The course consists of small group discussions of moral dilemmas, accompanied by lectures and readings designed to raise basic issues in moral philosophy and in the psychology of personal development. Kohlberg's theory of moral development has attracted great attention because of the intellectual heft behind his research and writing. Moral judgment, to Kohlberg, is reflected in the quality of the student's reasoning, not in the particular position adopted.

Reasoning would appear to be at the heart of the educational process, no less so in the areas of morality than in the career areas of one's discipline. Just as we do not expect the student in mathematics to become proficient without practice in solving problems, so we should not expect students to develop skills in moral reasoning without practice in thinking about moral dilemmas. There is really nothing radical about Kohlberg's cognitive approach to moral reasoning. Pitting one's reason and communicative skills against peers, teachers, and the best thinking of the ages is not a far-out educational idea.

One great myth holds that students should practice thinking about abstract problems, free of implications for real living. So ingrained is this myth that the word *academic* is defined in the dictionary as "having no practical or useful significance." To say that a question is academic is to dismiss it as having no practical value. We have not traveled far since the 1920s, when high school students were taught Latin to improve their English. With a little common sense and a lot of research, we finally discovered that there is little transfer of training and that studying English is the best way to learn English. But Latin did not disappear as a requirement without loud protests and considerable wringing-of-hands over the erosion of academic standards in the high schools.

It is now quite clear that the ability to solve academic problems bears little or no relationship to the ability to solve real-world problems. The correlation between college grades and adult success in life, however measured, is almost nil. Even as our catalogue statements continue to hope for students who can solve real problems, our teaching curriculum continues to hope, despite ample evidence to the contrary, that transfer of training does exist—that students who master the academic curriculum will be adequately prepared to master the challenges of life.

There is no conceivable reason why students should not practice thinking by thinking about real problems. Not only are real problems every bit as intellectually challenging as academic problems, they are frequently more appealing and motivating to students; thus, they often call forth more and better efforts. Why shouldn't our colleges be requiring students to present articulate arguments for and against such major and meaty issues as the graduated income tax, police review boards, automation, unionism, guaranteed income, egocentric hedonism, pollution, the death penalty? Each of these provides ample scope for exercising those skills that we say we most want students to develop—marshalling evidence, analyzing facts, presenting logical arguments, synthesizing information, communicating convictions.

Even though educators may recognize the problems of traditional curricula,[5] it is exceedingly difficult for them to make changes in curricular content. Such changes may be the most problemmatic of all innovations. No graduate schools turn out faculty members prepared to think with sophistication about the teaching of undergraduates; there is no reward structure that recognizes the huge effort it takes to prepare current and challenging materials; and innovators and their innovations are usually imposed upon a system that is ill-prepared to accommodate them. Nevertheless, a number of institutions have found creative solutions to curricular reform.

The most drastic solution creates a new institution that has no traditions to change. It may either be a cluster experimental college, independent of the parent university's requirements, or a new campus free to design its own structure. Evergreen State College in Washington, for example, strongly defended the position that education should emphasize problem-solving through interdisciplinary study, internships, and learning contracts. Since the administrators believe that the traditions of academic departments, tenure, and faculty rank do not contribute to those educational goals, they do not exist at Evergreen.

Some institutions have taken less drastic routes to curricular reform. Worcester Polytechnic Institute has managed to convert a quite traditional engineering curriculum into a new curriculum in which up to one-quarter of the student's work is done through projects and independent study on real-life problems.[6] An even less drastic change is the plan at MIT whereby small "research families" of faculty and students work together on real problems in the disciplinary fields.[7] Although I have been critical of discipline-obsessed curricula, I recognize that there are real problems to

[5]K. Patricia Cross, "New Students in a New World," in D. W. Vermilye, ed., *The Future in the Making: Current Issues in Higher Education 1973* (San Francisco: Jossey-Bass, 1973).

[6]S. Monroe, "WPI's Program for Technological Humanists," *Change*, June 1974, *6*(5), 20-23.

[7]G. W. Bonham, "Revitalizing Undergraduate Learning," *Change*, December-January, 1974-1975, *6*(10), 11-12; 63.

be found in the disciplinary fields. The fault lies not so much with the disciplines themselves as with traditional teaching that assumes the business of education is to provide answers rather than to stimulate questions and thought.

Another increasingly common approach that helps students cope with real-life problems stresses cooperative education and experiential learning. These task-oriented learning strategies have brought a fresh breeze of reality to some musty classrooms. And even though students too often have to figure out for themselves the relationship between on-campus study and off-campus internships, they are quite likely to rate their experiential learning as the richest of their college experience.

Competency-based curricula are yet another modification of traditional curricula, and they are more in tune with catalogue goals. Alverno College in Milwaukee, Wisconsin, expects each student to develop an awareness of the world in which she lives, and scores on a current events test are not an adequate demonstration of that competency. Rather, the college assesses the student's ability to carry on an intelligent conversation about contemporary affairs with four or five other adults. If I were a student at Alverno, awareness of the criteria for evaluation would certainly affect how I studied and what I learned about the world in which I live. I believe the learning curriculum can be changed through changing evaluation procedures.

Hundreds of examples could be given of institutional as well as individual efforts to make the undergraduate curriculum more meaningful, lively, and active for students. Indeed the trend in curricular innovations today is almost always student-centered. But for every person who bothers to think analytically and creatively about what we are teaching and why, there are a hundred who take the path of least resistance, content to go along with tradition and the status quo. Unfortunately, H. F. Gallup is quite right when he observes that "Dull lectures can follow dull lectures like dominoes; grading on a curve can occur *ad infinitum*; students can be bored in a lock-step system; all manner of inefficient and perhaps harmful teaching can take place. And if such teaching is part of the *status quo* it goes unchallenged, except perhaps by a few alienated students. The innovator does not go unchallenged."[8]

[8]H. F. Gallup, "Problems in the Implementation of a Course in Personalized Instruction," in J. G. Sherman, ed., *Personalized System of Instruction: 41 Germinal Papers* (Menlo Park, Ca.: W. A. Benjamin, 1974).

Indeed he or she does not. But bright and able faculty members and administrators are being recruited to the growing ranks of those interested in student-centered reform of the curriculum. The education of the 1970s and 1980s is not the education of the 1950s and 1960s. In the decades just past, we were primarily concerned about access to educational opportunity. We were so busy seeing that everyone—minorities, women, part-time students—had the opportunity to learn at minimal levels that we gave little attention to *maximizing* learning. Whereas the goal of the 1950s and 1960s was to achieve education for *all*, the goal of the 1970s and 1980s must be to achieve education for *each*. That can only be done through student-centered reform of the curriculum.

Faculty Roles in
Contract Learning

A. Paul Bradley, Jr.

Empire State College (ESC) is a statewide college without a campus.[1] It differs from other academic institutions in four ways. First, each student's degree program is shaped by the educational objectives of both the student and the college. At most institutions, student objectives are not a determining factor in the curriculum. Second, the elements of the learning contracts, which are the building blocks of the degree program, are formulated by the student with the advice and consent of faculty at ESC. In

[1]This chapter reports on "Developing Cost/Effectiveness Models for Postsecondary Education," a project partially funded by the Health, Education and Welfare Fund for the Improvement of Postsecondary Education. The project director is Ernest G. Palola.

traditional programs, the mode and pace of learning are fixed by the institution. Third, student learning contracts draw on the vast learning resources of the state, including tutors, work-study opportunities, internships, courses at other institutions, museums, and libraries. At most institutions, classroom instruction is the primary teaching mode. Fourth, ESC recognizes and credits documented prior learning regardless of how that learning came about. Most institutions have no provisions for recognizing prior informal learning.

In 1973, the Empire State College Office of Research and Evaluation conducted intensive interviews with all faculty members (the mentors) as well as with other staff at the regional centers to learn about the mentor role. In 1974, a mentor questionnaire was developed and administered to supplement the subjective interview findings. Results of the study and an evolving theory of nontraditional faculty development will be presented in a forthcoming monograph entitled *Mentor: An Emerging Faculty Role*.

Here are a few pertinent statistics about the college: Empire has eighty-six full-time mentors with thirty to be added in 1975-1976. As a group, the mentors seem to represent a fairly typical faculty. The average age is forty with a range from twenty-six to sixty-two; one-third are women; 59 percent have doctorates. Although the mentors have had, on the average, four years teaching experience in traditional settings, many have held positions outside education—examples include a director of a settlement house, a labor leader, a publisher, a newspaper reporter, a sales manager, a museum curator, and a printer. Furthermore, high percentages of respondents stated such personal goals as: "more direct, personal, individual contact with students" (97 percent); "learn to work better with a variety of learning resources both within and outside of the College" (84 percent); "work more with adult, experienced population" (76 percent); "learn to work better with students outside my discipline" (70 percent). Thus, although they appear to be typical on the surface, the mentors are a somewhat uncommon group of faculty members.

One of the major functions of mentors is advising students by meeting with them in face-to-face conferences. Such conferences enhance the possibility of personal, vocational, and academic counseling. Mentors also help students untangle intricacies in ESC procedures and bureaucracy by acting as ombudsmen.

Although some are uncomfortable interacting so closely with students, most mentors strongly endorse the importance of this aspect of the role.

A second function of mentors is to help students develop intellectually. Faculty have generally done this either by acting as "tutor" or as "facilitator." In the former mode, the mentor is the primary learning resource. The facilitator, on the other hand, uses a variety of learning resources—fellow mentors, faculty and courses at other institutions, internships, work-study, SUNY Independent Study courses, ESC learning modules—and teaches in response to student questions. Most mentors tend to favor the facilitator mode.

A third major function is for mentors to serve as evaluators. In committee, they review student degree programs, portfolios for advanced standing, and candidacy for graduation. However, most of a mentor's evaluative work is concerned with student performance in learning contracts. This process involves criticizing papers, holding face-to-face discussions, and completing the digest and evaluation forms that become part of the permanent record. Some mentors report that they are uneasy about this aspect of their role because there is little precedent for determining the criteria by which work is evaluated.

The development of the college is a fourth function of mentors, even though faculty involvement in college development both at the local and state levels has been difficult to achieve at times. One reason for the difficulty at ESC is that more than two years passed before the by-laws were approved and implemented. In addition, the statewide campus concept has created geographical difficulties. For example, only two all-college meetings are held a year (though many smaller gatherings are arranged for representatives from different parts of the college). Mentors may feel more loyalty to their local center or unit than to the college as a whole. Contributing to the overall governance problem is what J. J. Corson called the "enigma" of faculty involvement in decision-making: a comprehensive claim of competence on the one hand, and reticence to participate on the other.[2] Because widespread participation is essential to a dynamic "professional organization," the

[2] J. J. Corson, *Governance of Colleges and Universities* (New York: McGraw-Hill, 1960).

college must continue its attempts to find the appropriate level for mentor involvement in governing and planning.

Many mentors expressed concern over opportunities for them to continue to develop professionally at Empire. As a result, the college has set aside several weeks when mentors are not expected to meet with students. In addition, many mentors are now receiving professional leaves to travel, to help develop self-study learning modules, or to plan short-term residencies. Because a nontraditional faculty member must be prepared to work effectively with students in a variety of areas, opportunities for professional development are imperative.

The interviews predominately found that mentors are committed to their students and to being effective. Five problem areas were also uncovered by the interviews and further examined in the mentor questionnaire: concern over workload, concern over professional development, problems with identifying and tapping learning resources, concern over mentor role in decision-making, and anxiety. The questionnaire clearly demonstrated that the first four concerns are continuing ones. However, overall anxiety among mentors seems to be lessening.

Secondary analysis provided additional information in three areas. First, as student load increases so does concern over workload and professional development. Second, mentors with little previous experience in traditional institutions are the ones who are likely to identify problems in using external learning resources; this may indicate that younger mentors are more likely to try to "facilitate," while older mentors, with greater experience to draw upon, are more likely to "tutor." Third, less satisfied mentors tend to mention problems with learning resources and with their role in decision-making. Overall satisfaction was not statistically related to such dimensions as a mentor's regional learning center, years of experience, student load, or reasons for coming to Empire.

Perhaps a theory of faculty development for Empire State and other nontraditional institutions may be evolved by considering the stages through which faculty attracted to such institutions pass. First, faculty are attracted to nontraditional colleges by a philosophy stressing concern for students as individuals. Conversely, these faculty reject certain traditional educational practices. Of the respondents to the mentor questionnaire, 67 percent said that they came to the college because of "dissatisfaction with traditional programs." In some cases, this dissatisfaction can lead to personal distrust of anything disciplinary and structured— including tests, grades, majors, distribution requirements, faculty rank distinctions, regular class schedules, and course and program plans. Many faculty at Empire vehemently defend the organic exploratory contract in which a student and mentor make weekly decisions on what to study until the student finds a particular interest.

Although it is useful for faculty to shed certain vestiges of their previous teaching styles, the "antitraditionalism" stage is essentially nonconstructive. After abandoning old forms, faculty find it difficult to build new ones, partly because they are suspicious about anything that looks like a "traditional" structure. Further, the practice of operating by faculty consensus makes decision-making an arduous, a painstaking, and—for some—an unhappy process. One observer reported: "Recently, I witnessed their [faculty] delay and finally [their] abandonment of a crucial question: Fairhaven's academic direction, its goals and needs. Conversation on this important topic took four hours, was often gifted, even cogent, but it was indecisive to a fault."[3]

In consensus situations, almost any strongly held opinion tends to block action. Another reason why new structures are created slowly, as Ralph and Freedman point out, is that "administrative energies are likely to be focused on resolving the reciprocal antagonisms and stereotyping between the parent college and the innovative college, trying to explain the new college to the parent administration, board of trustees, evaluating committees, and the surrounding community and, similarly, to explain the actions of these bodies to members of the innovative college. Little time and energy are left for developing internal procedures and structures."[4] Thus, because of the "vengeance" with which nontraditional faculty discard old forms, a sense of immobility can easily permeate the college.

The second stage in faculty development at nontraditional

[3]Gary MacDonald, ed., *Five Experimental Colleges: Bensalem, Antioch-Putney, Franconia, Old Westbury, Fairhaven* (New York: Harper and Row, 1973).

[4]Norbert Ralph and Mervin Freedman, "Innovative Colleges: Challenge to Faculty Development," *New Directions for Higher Education*, 1973, no. 1, 69-82.

colleges might be called estrangement. The sense of immobility described above will disturb some, especially those less tolerant of ambiguity. Others find that students demand too much of their time, leaving few hours for individual scholarly activities. This saturated feeling was noted often in the interviews and on the mentor questionnaire. What is particularly draining for mentors is the great number of one-to-one contacts with students (four students a day, five days a week) plus the paperwork contract learning demands. As unfinished paperwork piles up, harsh feelings toward the Saratoga Springs Coordinating Center bureaucracy seem to increase. A third factor leading to estrangement is that all faculty, regardless of their expectations, are "quite unprepared for the environment" and are surprised and disappointed.[5] They experience an educational culture shock. Even faculty members with a student-oriented teaching style, while likely to do well in a nontraditional setting, sometimes find themselves overburdened because of their own accessibility. Others discover that their style and interests are more traditional than they thought. For them, innovation can be especially unsettling.

Ralph and Freedman suggest that "despite intentions to the contrary, most faculty continue to teach in fairly standard ways."[6] Although teaching in standard ways is difficult at Empire with its reliance on one-to-one relationships, the earlier observations about tutoring as opposed to facilitating, plus the appearance of group studies at the regional learning centers, seem to support the contention. However, traditional ways do not fit well overall into the unconventional settings.

Estrangement results in a few faculty feeling bitter and negative toward the new setting. Other mentors suffer a loss of self-esteem and confidence in their ability to handle the work, and they question whether they were wise to come to the nontraditional setting. During this time, many procrastinate on duties and fall behind in their work. In turn, this intensifies the bitterness. For example, one of the serious problems for students continues to be the sometimes lengthy delays between completing learning contracts and mentors filing "Digest and Evaluation" forms. As the pile of late "Digests and Evaluations" grows, there seems to be

[5] Ralph and Freedman.
[6] Ralph and Freedman.

a greater tendency for a mentor to lash out at the bureaucracy of the Coordinating Center.

Most faculty members overcome the anxieties of the estrangement stage by confronting two discomforting prospects—either changing their behavior or returning to traditional programs. Many change behavior by relinquishing their role as sole authority. In some institutions, this results in team teaching or consulting students when designing courses. At Empire, it means that mentors use tutors and other resources rather than relying primarily on themselves as experts. It also means sharing authority with students in developing degree programs and in deciding content and evaluation procedures on contracts. This self-confrontation stage is brief, but it is also intensive and exciting. At this time, mentors must weigh their personal needs and interests and decide whether to leave the nontraditional setting or to redirect their teaching style. They must examine their educational philosophy, commitment to students, commitment to a discipline, and career orientation. Though Empire State has not experienced the high turnover rates of some innovative programs, a few mentors have departed. One stated: "I simply found out that what I really like is conducting research."

The change from traditional teaching techniques to student-oriented methods occurs one step at a time. For some, change may begin even before they arrive at the nontraditional institution. Gradually, faculty create personal mentoring models that seem to work for them. Most important, "they become sensitive to the character-developing functions of teaching and to personal development as well as academic achievement."[7] They reorient themselves through the daily trial-and-error of personalized instruction that focuses on the whole person. At Empire, this is characterized by more rigorous evaluation and increased use of tutors, adjuncts, and such learning resources as internships, courses at other institutions, and work-study. In addition, mentors at this stage firmly defend learning that occurs outside the classroom as legitimate.

An important component of this fourth stage is the institutional environment. Just as the faculty member's own modus operandi is becoming more consistent and coherent, so is that of the institution. Procedures, evaluation standards, resources—all are

[7]Ralph and Freedman.

developing. This helps reduce confusion and, with it, tension. The environment becomes more organized, but it is structured differently from the traditional programs the faculty are trying to leave behind.

The fifth stage of development is renewal. Jose Ortega y Gasset felt that the "organization of higher education must be based on the student (not the professor or knowledge). Its two dimensions are: (1) what he [the student] is, a being of limited capacity, and (2) what he needs to know in order to live his life."[8] In a stage of renewal, the faculty member does not distinguish between cognitive and affective goals and is concerned simply with the student as a growing person. The teacher now has a personal, unified, but dynamic philosophy and style of teaching that links the isolated experience models identified as successful in stage four. The philosophy is modified as new experiences are gained, yet it remains cohesive. By the time mentors reach stage five, they usually have a strongly positive self-image. They are interested in reexamining current models regularly, exchanging experiences with fellow mentors, and experimenting with new techniques. Some may wish to develop written learning modules that can be used by all ESC students. Others may wish to video tape mentoring sessions with students. All are concerned with achieving the full potential of their students and themselves.

It is unclear whether the five stages of development apply only to the original faculty of a nontraditional program or whether people who join later also go through these stages. Currently, the pattern seems to apply to both groups; for example, procedures at Empire are increasingly well understood by the experienced mentors who helped create them, but to new mentors, these same procedures are often confusing. An evolutionary development seems to be necessary before the new faculty can understand, accept, and adjust to the procedures.

It is important to recognize the five stages of innovative faculty development so that steps can be taken to accelerate the process. For example, a mentor orientation program can be developed to make the uncommon procedures and requirements of mentoring more comprehensible from the beginning. In addition,

[8] Jose Ortega y Gasset, *The Mission of the University* (New York: W. W. Norton, 1944).

local administrators—deans and associate deans—can focus on recognizing symptomatic behavior and helping new mentors through uncomfortable times. Finally, new and prospective mentors themselves can profit from understanding the special problems—and the special rewards—they are likely to encounter.

Strategies for
Contract Learning

Jack Lindquist

Contract learning means that a student develops an individual learning program in collaboration with a "mentor" or small committee instead of by following a series of requirements laid out in the catalog.[1] The student and one or more faculty member negotiate a contract. At institutions such as the University of

[1] Information for this essay was derived from case histories developed for the Strategies for Change and Knowledge Utilization Project on South Carolina and Wilmington, from data of the Office of Research and Evaluation at Empire State College, and from Neal Berte's thoughtful essay about New College in Neal Berte (ed.), *Innovations in Undergraduate Education: Selected Institutional Profiles and Thoughts about Experimentalism* (University: New College, University of Alabama, 1972).

South Carolina and Wilmington College, that contract covers a whole degree program. Most contract experiences are traditional classes taught by established departments. In other institutions such as Empire State College, contracts are developed every few months and include a wide range of learning experiences, particularly independent study. But why abandon a set curriculum and degree requirements for the individual learning contract? Because it satisfies at least four needs: the logistical problems of working, married adults; the strong motivation to learn what one needs or wants to learn; the concern to develop intellectual skills and lifelong learning habits; and the desire to individualize and personalize learning.

First, most contract learning students are older than the traditional age eighteen to age twenty-two college students. At Empire State, 63 percent are married, 60 percent work full-time, and only 3 percent are unemployed. When asked why they enrolled at Empire State, students responded that the flexibility and independence were especially attractive. They could keep their jobs and often use those jobs as learning laboratories. The same reasoning applied to taking care of the kids and spouse. Empire State students are very interested in gaining credit for what is often impressive informal learning. As the postsecondary population bulge gets older, we will increasingly need to provide learning opportunities that can occur around and in adult responsibilities.[2] Assessing students' prior learning is controversial and need not be part of a contract learning program, but if adult students are to be well-served, it should be considered.

Second, although many academic practices do not reflect the fact, it is no secret that people learn best what they *want* to learn, what seems useful to them. Contract learning students report that they are attracted to this approach because they can build learning programs that reflect their own interests. At Empire State, 65 percent of the students have quite clear learning objectives in mind when they first enroll. Contract learning does not necessarily mean students will choose very narrow programs with no tough or foreign subjects, however. Nor does it mean that stu-

---

[2] George Weathersby, *Future Policy Issues Concerning Postsecondary Education Supply and Demand* (Cambridge: Harvard Graduate School of Education, 1974).

dents will avoid learning experiences that do not seem immediately practical and relevant. Of course, such problems can result, and state education officials identified them at Empire State. But persuasion research consistently finds that personal interaction with respected individuals is the best way to move people from one view to another, from one behavior to another.[3] Coercion works as long as one has power over another, but its effect greatly diminishes when control is released—as at graduation. Mentors or small committees, in the course of building a personal relationship with a student, can nudge the student out of narrow interests into related but broader learning so that motivation to learn accompanies liberal exposure. Institutions or individual faculty members plagued by students who do not seem interested in anything being taught would do well to try the contract approach.

The third need has been consistently expressed by faculty members who have completed the *Institutional Goals Inventory.*[4] They feel that preparing students in academic subjects is highly important and fairly successfully accomplished. Developing intellectual skill—problem solving, scientific inquiry, learning how to learn, developing habits of lifelong learning—is rated even higher but is regarded as far less effectively accomplished. One reason may be that traditional teaching methods emphasize the professor giving information and the student listening, taking notes, memorizing, and feeding back on tests.[5] Conversely, a survey at Empire State reveals that students spend most of their study time in "higher" mental activities: analysis, synthesis, evaluation, and application. Recurring conferences between mentor and student, constant application of book learning to work or family, field assignments, and emphasis on self-evaluation of learning probably are some of the reasons for this much different emphasis. The sharp boundaries between "real life" and the classroom disappear. Thus, contract learning, appears to be an attractive alternative for many faculty, administrators, and students who wish to do a better job at intellectual development.

[3]Ralph Rosnow and Edward Robinson, *Experiments in Persuasion* (New York: Academic Press, 1967).

[4]Richard Peterson, *Goals for California Higher Education: A Survey of 116 College Communities* (Berkeley: Educational Testing Service, 1973).

[5]Arthur Chickering, "Undergraduate Academic Experience," *Journal of Educational Psychology* 63 (1972), 134-143.

The fourth need met by contract learning is one faculty increasingly face as admissions become more open: the enormous range of student interests, skills, learning styles, learning rates, and self-confidence. Audio-Tutorial, the Personalized System of Instruction, and Computer Assisted Instruction are ways to individualize learning rate and give attention to developing skills and self-confidence. But they tend to be limited to what the professor determines will be covered; they also face the limitations of standardized design and costly, sometimes uncooperative, machines.[6] The learning contract, because it is a human interaction with a high degree of flexibility in adapting to individual needs, has great potential for personalizing learning. Of course, it still requires a professor who can respond to widely divergent interests, skills, styles, learning rates, and self-concepts. Contract learning faculty do find their role extremely complex and demanding. But, as Empire State evidence reveals, instructors can meet the challenge.

Any attempt to introduce contract learning on a campus will need the support of various authorities, funding sources, and especially faculty. The following notions, drawn from my observations of several institutions considering contract learning, deal with the kinds of support and resistance that might be expected.

One source of support would be persons worried about declining enrollment figures. Contract learning programs attract all the students they can handle, primarily because adult students comprise an expanding postsecondary market. State officials, business officers, and even faculty concerned about personnel cutbacks might be expected to consider this potential enrollment aid. A second source of support could come from persons who value personalized education; student-oriented faculty, counselors, and teachers struggling with diverse classes might well be interested. Since students themselves rate their own personal and intellectual development as extremely important,[7] they too should be attracted to the idea. Third, most faculty probably would be interested in an approach that emphasizes intellectual development. Fourth, persons generally concerned about the education of adults, such as continuing education staff, might be supportive if they were included in the program.

[6]Ernest House, *Politics of Educational Innovation* (Berkeley: McCutchan, 1974).
[7]Peterson, *Goals for California Higher Education.*

Initially, the negative side of the ledger on contract learning is likely to be much longer than the positive side. First, although administrators and funding sources might like the increased enrollment possibilities, they will need to be convinced that the costs of all that personal attention will not be astronomical. Alternatives such as those undertaken by the University of South Carolina and Wilmington College, which do not include frequent mentor contact or development of new learning resources, may be necessary in the beginning. However, it must be noted that these programs sacrifice the strength of ongoing mentor-student interaction. Certainly, the extent to which a new program can tap existing learning resources, facilities, and personnel, and can maintain a mentor-student ratio close to that of traditional arrangements, is crucial.

Second, a major concern of faculty and credential authorizing agencies will be academic quality—the depth, breadth, and degree of learning. At South Carolina, the faculty became so suspicious of the quality of University Without Walls contracts that they eliminated the program. In contrast, the contract-based Bachelor of General Studies (BGS) program at the same institution relied on courses and grades in academic departments. It took a conservative academic posture, published evidence of high grade achievement by BGS students, and thereby earned the support of the faculty senate's watchdog committee. Empire State's nontraditional learning practices and evaluation procedures received close scrutiny by the Middle States Association, but it did grant accreditation, enthusiastically, in response to the college's first application. It is possible, therefore, to meet traditional concerns about academic quality with nontraditional means. But, as the slow acceptance of Individualized Educational Planning by faculty at Wilmington indicates, it is an obstacle toward which persuasive evidence must constantly be directed.

A third source of resistance can stem from interunit competition. Although Empire State's student body is quite different from the ones at other State University of New York campuses, some feel that the new program will hurt enrollments at these other campuses. At South Carolina, departments keep a wary eye on BGS enrollments even though all the FTE credit goes to the departments in which BGS students take their courses. Those in more traditional departments argue that BGS students can avoid normally required courses (no specific courses are required of them) and thereby weaken enrollments in such courses. In turn,

BGS advocates argue that many students would not be enrolled at all were it not for their program.

A fourth kind of resistance is common to all innovations: discomfort with the unknown.[8] Faculty, administrators, and students know their way around the current practices—perhaps too well. Mentoring appears as a very complex and demanding role to faculty who have done mostly classroom teaching, and it is. Only 12 percent of Empire State's faculty had prior experience in non-traditional teaching. Administrators might well worry about administering programs and supervising faculty under contract conditions. A further concern is that the personal responsibility for developing and carrying out one's own learning can be pretty disconcerting to students. Special task forces at Empire State are now tackling the problem of how to attract and help students who are less sure of their objectives and less ready for independent learning than most current Empire State students seem to be.

A fifth restraint is time. For persons already overworked, finding the hours necessary to develop a new program is not easy. Much time is needed to learn how to function in the mentor role, to meet all students individually, to prepare for what may appear to be thirty different courses, to write and review evaluations. Faculty at Empire State have found that the workload demands of this kind of education are formidable indeed.

Finally, there is the matter of rewards. Contract learning, like most teaching innovations, "does not pay." The faculty member is distracted from scholarly research and writing, pursuits that do pay in one way or another. Those who gain satisfaction from classroom performance find no classrooms in which to perform. The department and institution face a substantial problem in trying to develop the prestige that traditionally has attracted students and grants. The student worries that this degree will not be viewed as favorably as others by graduate schools and employers. It is also difficult to both personalize education and generate the FTEs necessary to get state funds or keep tuition within decent bounds. Contract learning institutions are meeting a good many of these concerns fairly well, but the problems persist. Faculty members at

---

[8]Goodwin Watson, "Resistance to Change," in Goodwin Watson, ed., *Concepts for Social Change* (Washington, D.C.: NTL Institute for Applied Behavioral Science, 1966).

Empire State and Wilmington report that they can barely keep up in their fields, let alone conduct productive research. Contract committee members at South Carolina get virtually no rewards except personal satisfaction for the additional time and skill they put into contracts with BGS students. The excitement of a new and meaningful innovation can sustain enthusiasts for a while, but then what?

With all these obstacles, plus a strong dose of organizational inertia, it is a wonder that such innovation exists anywhere. Yet it does. It is worth considering the strategies innovative programs have used to reduce resistance, increase support, and eventually launch working programs. At each institution with which I am familiar, a concerned authority first established a committee. Nothing surprising in that. The committees were largely composed of persons with strong interest in individualizing learning and with some expertise or experience in that area. These groups studied the local situation; considered research, theory, and practices elsewhere; and formulated proposals for change. Again, that is pretty standard procedure. The groups did seem to have better contacts with external knowledge resources than many committees do. South Carolina had an experienced University Without Walls leader, Warren Buford, on its committee and was most impressed by Bachelor of General Studies programs at the University of Iowa and the University of Michigan. The committee at the University of Alabama was regularly advised by the New College's eventual dean, Neal Berte, then on the staff of Ottawa University, a contract learning college. Arthur Chickering, who was experienced in the personalized program of Goddard College, was on the committee that designed Empire State; he later became its first academic vice president. Wilmington College benefited from interaction with Chickering, Goddard's founder Royce Pitkin, and by Philip Young, the college's ombudsman, who visited Ottawa and who later became director of Individualized Educational Planning. Thus, even though each group was building a program uniquely fitted to local conditions, it did not hesitate to benefit from the experiences and expertise of others. The wheel was more adapted and modified than reinvented.

It is one thing for a committee to lock itself away, become knowledgeable about a subject, and generate a proposal. It is quite another for anyone else to buy that proposal. At the two institutions with which I am most familiar, South Carolina and Wilmington, it took quite a bit of effort to reduce resistance, particularly among faculty. The South Carolina committee was an ad hoc group formed by the university president. It and a previously established committee of associate deans spent the year of 1970-1971 developing a proposal. President Jones, who had once been criticized for innovating by decree, avoided that criticism by sending the committee's proposal to the faculty senate's Committee on Curricula and New Courses (CCNC). That body was chaired by a political scientist who expressed little interest in the low-achieving students or the nontraditional experimentation stressed in the proposal. But the CCNC complied with the recommendation in the proposal that an experimental college be created to house the BGS as well as other experimental programs. Unfortunately, it did so by grouping a program for disadvantaged students (called Opportunity Scholars), a semester-long independent study program (called Contemporary University), and the very controversial University Without Walls all under the same structural umbrella—without consulting the leaders of these programs. Not surprisingly, none of the other experimental programs wanted to be associated with UWW. In addition, many faculty members were suspicious that a large unit competitive with their departments was being formed, probably by the president. These concerns, plus questions about the academic respectability of BGS itself, spelled doom for the proposal, but an associate professor of psychology quickly rallied support to table the proposal in the October 1971 faculty senate meeting. The motion passed. During the next five months, this person and a few close associates who had become concerned about undergraduate education during the Kent State-Jackson State-Cambodia disasters organized a "Tuesday night discussion group." Their aims were to discuss alternative proposals with prominent members of the faculty senate and to inform faculty about the worthiness of a modified version of the original proposal. The president and provost drafted their own new proposal for a BGS degree. After negotiations with the Senate Committee on Curricula and New Courses, a final proposal was passed. Reflecting on the process, observers felt that the low visibility but consistent aid of the president, strong backing by the academically conservative and respected provost, and persuasion by the informal advocacy group saved the day. This view supports Mahan's finding that both executive initiative and widespread faculty involvement are necessary to innovation.[9] It also supports Rodgers and Shoemaker's contention that personal interaction that moves from innovators to open opinion leaders to their reference groups, as the Tuesday night group did, is vital.[10]

Wilmington took a different route to contract learning. Proposals for contract learning and a degree without specific requirements were presented to faculty by a standing committee, the Educational Policies Council, in spring 1972, but the faculty did not take action. The summer lull and the new issues in the fall put these ideas on the shelf. Meanwhile, the president and provost wrote position papers on the future of the college. They thought that such papers might catalyze faculty action to resolve the serious problem of attracting adequate enrollment. These papers were circulated and discussed in division meetings. Faculty members were irritated because they felt that traditional departmental offerings were being criticized for enrollment difficulties. They also disliked the suggestion that innovations emphasizing applied programs were needed. Admissions and public relations should do more, some faculty said, to publicize the academic strengths of the college.

Another executive strategy at Wilmington was to present survey data from the Institutional Goals Inventory and Strategies for Change in faculty retreats and workshops. The data did stimulate talk about the need to strengthen intellectual and personal development of students, but still no action. Then the ombudsman Philip Young returned from Ottawa University to share the approach of its president, Peter Armacost. Instead of alarming his faculty about the future by pushing certain changes, Armacost had entrusted the instructors with assessing the problem and developing solutions, and he also scraped up institutional monies to support their work. He transferred ownership of the change process to them. Heeding this example, the president and provost of Wilmington decided to host a series of "mini-retreats" for themselves and groups of a dozen faculty members from different departments.

[9]Don Mahan, "Control, Consensus and Change," *The Research Reporter* (Berkeley: Center for Research and Development in Higher Education, 1973).

[10]Everett Rodgers and F. Floyd Shoemaker, *Communication of Innovations: A Cross Cultural Approach* (New York: Free Press, 1971).

The purpose of these retreats would be to generate a plan for the future that faculty and trustees could adopt by consensus, which was the way decisions were usually made in that Quaker college. On the last day of March 1973, a decision was reached to implement the contract and open degree ideas proposed the year before. Again, those who look back at the situation say that key factors were the slow personal persuasion across departmental lines, steadfast support and initiative by executive administration but with faculty ownership, considerable data feedback and discussion, and a core of diligent advocates led by the ombudsman and several members of the Educational Policies Council.

At the University of Alabama, such support at the top, involvement below, and persistent advocacy could be cited as the keys to reducing resistance successfully. And the quiet but determined initiative and support of Chancellor Ernest Boyer has permitted advocates to launch the major experiment at Empire State. When the group that would have to implement the change, is granted control of the problem-solving process, as at Wilmington, another strategy well supported by a body of change theory is effectively employed.[11]

Change models, like the governing process, tend to stop at the decision to implement an innovation. But the decision may represent genuine commitment by only a few. Skills, understanding of objectives, facilities, time, leadership, rewards, early evaluation, and feedback to work out the bugs and convince the skeptics —all of these are yet to come.[12]

At Empire State and New College, leadership was delegated to two people who had a firm conceptual and experiential grasp on contract learning—Chickering and Berte. At Empire State, while Chickering and provost Loren Baritz began recruiting faculty and staff and getting the program launched, President James Hall, who had been on the Central Administration staff, began the same quiet process of building relationships with SUNY Central and concerned groups around the state. At New College, Berte immediately began to recruit resources as well as to explain the concepts behind New College to faculty, administrators, and students who

[11]Watson, "Resistance to Change."
[12]Neal Gross, Joseph Giacquinta, and Marilyn Bernstein, *Implementing Organizational Innovations* (New York: Harper and Row, 1973).

might have reason to resist the innovation. As Berte explains, he did not want to build, either intentionally or by default, an isolated enclave that would encourage rumors rather than understanding. Without support from its external environment, neither of these programs could have survived; and interpersonal contact was the principle means of gaining needed support.

Just as it is difficult to get a program approved unless the concerned groups are involved, so it is difficult to implement that program unless the faculty feel meaningfully involved. At Empire State, a faculty senate system was quickly developed; even though faculty still report feeling left out of some major decisions and are unhappy with the amount of time the committee system takes, collaborative decision-making is becoming more and more common. Collaborative decision-making is also the governing model at New College.

Another form of support is money. New College, Wilmington, and Empire State all launched contract learning with the help of sizeable foundation grants. Their experience certainly suggests that there is money available for promising programs. It also suggests that interpersonal relationships with leaders of grant-giving agencies (and legislators or donors) are most important. A key financial strategy, however, is to move personnel and other ongoing resources away from a dependence on grant money as soon as possible so that when or if the grant runs out, the institution will not have to bear an unrealistic burden.

In each institution mentioned above, an advisory committee was established, apparently for four reasons: to watchdog the program, to advise its leaders, to strengthen contact between the innovation and the wider community, and to involve outsiders so that isolated enclave would not result. For the committees at South Carolina and Wilmington, people knowledgeable about contract learning or those whom external faculty considered to be wise judges were sought.

South Carolina faced one problem by assuming a low profile. For several reasons, some influential faculty and administrators were suspicious of the quality of the contract learning program. It was initiated in part for students with weak performance records. It was part of the College of General Studies, which was known for coordinating the night school and a two-year degree program. It would be run by a blunt-speaking dean who was not regarded as "one of us" by disciplinary academicians. And some feared it would create a drain on departmental enrollments. To counter the uneasiness prompted by these reasons, the dean and his staff decided to play down the program. The BGS was not widely publicized. Staff carefully recruited a small initial group of students and closely watched their academic performance, which turned out to be excellent. Even today the program remains a quiet alternative despite its steady growth and the large number of applications.

Empire State also began quietly. Care was taken not to criticize traditional education. The new program was to supplement, not supplant, programs of existing institutions. It was to serve a new constituency unable to take advantage of existing opportunities rather than compete for the same kinds of students. It stressed academic quality translatable into traditional terms. And a large-scale research project was initiated so that educational effectiveness and related costs of the program could be measured systematically. Early data on student experiences, their satisfaction, and their success after graduation supported the contract learning approach and were much appreciated by the Middle States and New York state accrediting teams. These data also have been fed to administrative offices and self-study or planning groups to help them spot early problems.

Credible leadership, strong relations with sources of external support or resistance, and careful evaluation to meet the concerns of outsiders are all important. But the heart of contract learning is the contract relationship between faculty member and student. At Empire State, a productive relationship has been insured by recruiting faculty who are committed to the idea and who have experiences which might relate to the advising, tutoring, resource linking, coordinating, and evaluating tasks of a mentor.

No ongoing faculty development occurred during the first three years of Empire State, although short orientations were held. At New College, faculty development began with regular student evaluations of faculty. Faculty members who would participate in the three-person contract committees were assigned initially by deans or department chairpersons at South Carolina. I interviewed about half of these faculty participants at random in 1973 and learned that many knew almost nothing about the Bachelor of General Studies program when assigned, received only a brief orientation, hardly ever met as a full team because of scheduling problems, and in some cases had not laid eyes on their student advisees. There was no program to train them in the complex educational process of developing degree programs with students suitable to their needs, interests, and style. Over the last two years, a cadre of informed, experienced and interested faculty has been formed, but there is still no training available. At Wilmington, the three-faculty/one-student committees also are proving logistically unwieldy, although the committees that do get together find the experience and the resulting student contracts most promising. No formal faculty development program is available yet at Wilmington.

The new Center for the Improvement of Individualized Education at Empire State should help to solve the lack of faculty training. A major objective of this center is to build faculty development procedures and opportunities for persons involved in programs that have mentor and contract interactions. An early project brought mentors from various institutions together in order to clarify the mentoring role and develop ways to learn how to do it better.

Innovations, if they survive, quickly become part of the status quo. Procedures stabilize and the initial participants socialize new ones as to the way things are done. If the innovation is a subunit of a larger institution, as is each of the four institutions discussed here, its founders may think that eventually it will expand into the larger community; but it is more likely to settle into its corner of the campus or system. So, two questions arise: How can the things that work on one campus be disseminated more widely? And how can a program continuously renew itself?

There is not much evidence yet that Empire State has influenced the educational process in the rest of the SUNY system, although the college has attracted considerable national attention. A proposal of an Empire State task force suggests that mentors be formally aligned with nearby SUNY or CUNY departments, not only to enable them to enjoy the stimulation of colleagues in their own fields but also to allow the methods of Empire State to become more widely known.

New College, on the other hand, is having an impact on the rest of the University of Alabama, particularly through its professors. Berte reports that when faculty members return to their original departments, they take their innovative ways with them. In this case, close interaction and overlapping membership has helped spread the innovation.

As for renewal, Empire State recently launched a broad, participative planning project called the President's Committee on College Development. Early task force reports stress that it is committed both to refine current programs and to tackle new populations and new approaches so that the college can meet its goal of serving diverse student needs. Empire State also has established what is essentially an institutional renewal wing consisting of the Center for Improving Individualized Education, the Office of Research and Evaluation, and Policy Analysis and Evaluation officers. Such services are as nontraditional as the college and require support. Innovation was not initiated without substantial investment in time and resources, and there is no evidence to suggest that renewal will come any more cheaply.

Another major problem in implementing innovations concerns workload and rewards. Faculty members at Empire State report that their endurance is stretched by all the things required to build and maintain personalized learning experiences for a steady influx of students. And then there is the considerable time it takes to help develop the program and college in general. Professional scholarship can suffer. Although most mentors at Empire State report they are not worried about career opportunities, and although the promotion-tenure reward system recognizes the mentoring activity, professors are concerned about keeping abreast of developments in their fields. Essentially, time spent serving on contract committees at South Carolina and Wilmington is time subtracted from activities that departments and the profession reward. Contract learning, like most innovations, is extremely demanding and nontraditional in its functions. The danger is that without time to meet the demands and rewards suitable to the functions, implementors soon may lose their enthusiasm for the enterprise.

In conclusion, several strategies for implementing contract learning are suggested by the experiences of the four institutions described above. First, a committee should be launched to study local goals and needs and to adapt contract learning (if that is the solution which fits) to those conditions. It should include persons knowledgeable about contract learning and the local situation as well as persons respected by those who must support an eventual proposal. This group and concerned outsiders should have access to evidence about local conditions and to external knowledge resources. Evidence particularly worth gathering pertains to costs, quality and acceptance, difficulty, time, and rewards.

Second, broad support should be obtained from a core of persistent advocates. Support should begin at the top of the institution but should involve faculty so that the problem-solving process is basically theirs. Persons whose support is needed should be persuaded by personal interaction and quiet diplomacy. Collaboration should occur across interest groups and advisory groups that link the innovation to sources of external advice and concern should be formed. Implementing faculty should be involved in developing the program as soon as possible.

Third, external funding is a good way to get things rolling, but stable internal support should be developed as quickly as possible.

Fourth, leaders and faculty should be chosen who understand the program, are committed to its objectives and methods, and have appropriate background for advising, tutoring, coordinating, collaborative evaluating, and learning the resource linkage skills they need. Those who must assume the complex new roles involved in contract learning will need opportunities for orientation and professional development. They will also need a reasonable workload (not a greater burden than traditional approaches) and suitable rewards for mentoring functions. Finally, there must be careful evaluation of contract learning experiences, outcomes, and related costs both to aid external judges (accreditors, funding groups, governance bodies) and to spot implementation problems before they become insurmountable. If the innovation should be disseminated, mechanisms must be set up to do this. The dissemination process must allow time, expertise, and rewards for external interaction, for conference reporting, and for applying the innovation in other places. Renewal units such as planning committees, research offices, faculty development centers, policy analysis and planning officers should be established. Everyone else will quickly get buried in business as usual.

The above is hardly a complete list. But I think that both change research and the cases described here support the importance of these strategies. If these approaches are added to the wisdom of individual experience, contract learning—or other worthy innovations aimed at personalizing higher education—can become a reality at any institution.

9

New Approaches to Improve Teaching

Jerry G. Gaff

There is every indication that the phrase, "publish or perish," popularized by Caplow and McGee in their class study, *The American Marketplace,* soon will be regarded as a quaint piece of academic nostalgia that characterized the 1950s and 1960s. We will miss the phrase when we don't have it to kick around any more because it has figured in much campus humor. For instance, George Meany reportedly remarked, on first hearing that professors were expected to publish or perish: "It's too bad so many chose the wrong alternative." And there is the story of two deans who met at a conference; one boasted to the other that his faculty had resolved the conflict between research and teaching. When pressed for details about how they had managed this feat, he confessed: "They do neither."

Most colleges and universities are affirming the primacy of teaching rather than research. Faced with the prospects of leveling student enrollments, declining faculty positions, and becoming "tenured in," most institutions are coming to realize that they will have to rely on their current faculty to provide fresh perspectives, infuse new ideas, and give leadership to innovative programs if they expect to maintain vigorous educational climates in the years ahead. Faculty members, too, find the going tough. In the midst of the tightest job market in memory, they are finding it difficult to get positions, to change jobs, or even to obtain tenure at their institutions. Increasingly, faculty careers will be confined to one institution, and faculty will have to look to that one school to provide the enriching experiences they need to grow professionally and personally.

New approaches to faculty development are emerging to cope with these changing conditions. Professional development for faculty is not new; opportunities for sabbatical leaves, travel to conferences and meetings, and research support have long been available, albeit often at modest levels. What *is* new is that these traditional forms are being supplemented by more specific efforts to help professors grow and develop in their teaching roles. Centers, divisions, offices, and programs have been established to provide services variously referred to as instructional development, learning resources, faculty development, teaching improvement, professional development, or organizational development. They have been established by every kind of college and university as well as by state systems, consortia, and associations. These centers and offices include both small and large scale efforts; their programs range from narrow, specialized ones to broad, comprehensive ones; and they engage in a wide variety of activities.

These new enterprises are still in the formative stage. Improving the quality of instruction has been like the weather—everybody talks about it but nobody does anything about it. But today, new concepts of instructional improvement are being advanced and new programs are providing opportunities for faculty members to enhance one or more aspects of their teaching.

Academic folklore has held that "a teacher is born, not made," and that "teaching is an art, not a science." These sayings imply that little can be done to bring about the improvement of instruction. Because they have become interwoven with the concept of academic freedom, many instructors believe that "a professor's classroom is his castle," and that it is somehow unprofessional for one faculty member to criticize, offer suggestions, or even observe another in his classroom. These injunctions have made it difficult for professors to learn about teaching from one another, and thus one opportunity by which they might improve their instruction has been circumvented. Although these views may have been useful in the past, the old saw that "a university should hire good people and get out of their way" is a hollow slogan when student enrollment dips, faculty positions are trimmed, and even the future of some institutions is threatened.

As traditional concepts have been called into question, new concepts of faculty development are taking their place. It is now assumed that teaching is a learned configuration of knowledge, attitudes, values, motivations, skills, and sensitivities, and that with additional learning in these areas faculty may become more effective instructors. In-service programs consisting of seminars, workshops, individual or group projects, or consultations are helping faculty members enhance and extend their instructional competencies and increase their satisfaction with their work.

Most of the new programs for professional development rest upon certain assumptions and propositions, which together constitute a conceptual framework for these endeavors. One assumption is that faculty members are the most important educational resource of a college or university. Just as material resources must be given special care and attention to enhance their value, so the talents, interests, and skills of faculty must be systematically cultivated.

Faculty development programs also assume that teaching is the primary, though by no means the only, professional activity of most faculty members. A major reason why instructors choose to work in a college or university is their commitment to teaching, and most faculty members want to excel in this activity. Scholarship and research—another major professional activity of many faculty members—need not be antithetical to effective teaching. Ways can and should be found to allow research to enrich and complement teaching. Teaching has been slighted by academic tradition. In most schools, this neglect has not been due to lack of interest among individual faculty members. Rather, it can be traced to factors pervading the general academic culture, such as the lack of preparation for teaching roles during graduate education, the absence of in-service education compared to that found in other professions, and the paucity of academic policies (in the areas of promotion, salary, tenure) to provide positive support and reward for effective teaching.

Although there is little systematic evidence about the quality of teaching and learning in most institutions, it is generally assumed, both within and outside academe, that it may be improved. Improving the quality of instruction requires working with administrators and students—perhaps even with members of the larger community—as well as with faculty members. All of these groups have legitimate interest in, and responsibility for, making the instructional program work well. Just as faculty members receive little preparation for their instructional roles, administrators have little training for the leadership, policy formulation, administrative, and managerial roles of their work. Department chairpersons, deans, vice presidents, and presidents—no less than faculty members—need to develop professionally, and furthermore, they need to encourage and support the growth of the individuals in their charge.

Teaching is a complex set of attitudes, knowledge, skills, motivations, and values. The improvement of instruction and learning requires an awareness of the complex relationship among faculty, students, and institutions. Practically, this means that there is no single method of effective teaching or learning; simplistic solutions or proposals advanced as panaceas with a doctrinaire approach should be avoided.

In recognizing the complexity of the teaching-learning process, proponents of instructional improvement also recognize the great diversity among students. Their various learning styles are based on differences in ability, interest, educational background, future aspirations, and personality orientations, and these different learning styles call for different kinds of learning experiences.

Faculty members, too, are a diverse lot. They vary on such key factors as age, field of specialization, teaching experience, and educational philosophy. Because diversity is one of the greatest strengths of any faculty, every effort should be made to assist individual faculty members in ways that are consistent with their particular values, needs, and personal styles, and that are also consistent with student needs and institutional goals. Lasting change can only be brought about by supporting and reinforcing positive efforts of faculty members. Intrinsic interest rather than extrinsic demand is what leads individuals to seek improvement. Finally, participation in faculty development activities must be on a voluntary basis if enduring improvement is to be obtained.

Although all instructional improvement programs are designed to raise the quality of teaching and learning, these programs vary considerably. Depending on what aspects of the teaching-learning process they emphasize, they may be categorized in one of three ways: as instructional development, faculty development, or organizational development. Each category draws on different intellectual traditions, makes different analyses about what ails teaching and learning, and prescribes different solutions.

Instructional development focuses on how conditions of learning are designed, particularly in relation to *courses*. The intellectual roots for this program lie in the fields of curriculum and instruction, learning theory, educational media and technology, and systems theory. The instructional developer assists a faculty member, or a team of teaching faculty, to specify measurable cognitive and affective objectives of student learning, to design learning activities and materials relevant to those objectives, to measure student accomplishment, and to revise the instructional sequence and procedures in light of evaluation. One major strength of this approach is that it enables faculty members to tailor their instruction around the outcomes of learning for students rather than to merely cover the course content. In addition, the objectives, learning experiences, and evaluation of students' attainment of objectives are more systematically related. Thus, the probability that the objectives will be attained is increased.

Because it is easier to apply these concepts and techniques to a structured discipline, instructional development tends to be more readily accepted by faculty members in the natural sciences. Although the faculty in the humanities and social sciences generally are less attracted to the systematization of their courses, this approach has been profitably used in those fields as well.

Faculty development programs focus on *faculty members* rather than on the courses they teach. The intellectual roots of these programs lie in those disciplines that study human development over the life span, particularly developmental, clinical, and social psychology and psychiatry. The goal is to develop different instructional competencies for individual faculty members, and these competencies can be divided into six main areas.

The first area is *knowledge about higher education.* It is commonly asserted that faculty members lack such knowledge and that they need to be exposed to the professional literature and diverse practices of higher education. Some faculty development programs help faculty acquire this knowledge by inviting lecturers to analyze contemporary educational issues; forming formal and informal faculty discussion groups; collecting books, articles and reports; publishing a newsletter; or working with interested departments to incorporate substantive educational discussions into their faculty meetings.

A second area is *teaching skills.* Because some critics maintain that faculty members lack the skills to teach effectively whether in the classroom or out, several programs focus on helping faculty acquire appropriate skills and sensitivities. Workshops, video tapes of teaching episodes, and classroom visits have been used to help faculty develop specific communication skills, such as listening or questioning; develop sensitivities to such factors as affective tone and interpersonal dynamics in a classroom; improve common instructional strategies, such as preparing and delivering lectures and leading discussion groups; and adopt new instructional approaches, such as preparing learning contracts or serving as resource persons.

A third area is *feedback about their own teaching behavior.* Most people have only partial knowledge about how others perceive them. Some faculty believe that they might become better teachers if they had accurate and useful feedback from students, colleagues, and administrators about their teaching behavior. It is not uncommon today for faculty members to ask students to rate them on general qualities that are presumed to be indicative of effective teaching, but other techniques also have been used. Faculty members have recorded their classes with either video or audio tapes and have discussed the tapes with students and colleagues; rating scale items have been developed by individuals and departments that reflect specific concerns of those involved in teaching; and classroom visits have provided a means for obtaining useful feedback.

A fourth area of competence is *affective development.* Some critics argue that the main problem with teaching is that faculty members have not examined their attitudes, values, and assumptions with respect to what constitutes effective teaching, desirable relationships with students, or productive relationships with their colleagues. Since these attitudes have often been derived from the previous training, they may work in opposition to the needs of an instructor's current students, and even to his own satisfaction. Some institutions have held workshops that have encouraged faculty members to explore their attitudes and values about teaching and learning by means of task-oriented sensitivity groups, simulation and games, or mutual interviewing.

A fifth area is *awareness of other disciplines and the community*. A common charge leveled against academics is that they are encapsulated in narrow academic specializations and are unaware of important relationships with other fields of knowledge and the realities of the larger world. In order to promote contact among faculty members, cross-disciplinary seminars have been held, various kinds of interdisciplinary programs have been formed, team teaching has been encouraged, and experimental colleges have been created.

The sixth and last area of competence involves placing the emphasis on *learning rather than teaching*. Some analysts assert that the problem is not to have faculty work on improving their teaching but to become more sensitive to how and what students are learning. Distributing written materials and conducting seminars and workshops—often with cognitive, affective, and skill development components—help to acquaint faculty with the needs of students who vary on such factors as intellectual ability, social background, learning style, and personality orientation.

The third category of instructional development programs is *organizational development*. These programs focus on the organization within which faculty, students, and administrators work. The intellectual roots of this approach are found primarily in organizational theory and organizational change and group dynamics. Further, because the application of organizational development has received its greatest impetus in the world of business, it also has become intertwined with concepts of management.

One aim of this approach is to develop administrative and interpersonal competencies among leaders of the organization. Central administrators, department chairpersons, and faculty who play leadership roles are seldom prepared to administer or manage organizations, and they must learn a variety of concepts, skills, and techniques relevant to this kind of professional responsibility. Discussions, workshops, and consultations are provided to help administrators and others clarify their attitudes, values, and assumptions regarding management of the organization; identify various leadership styles and develop the ones consistent with their personalities and the needs of the organization; clarify and establish organizational goals; plan and conduct meetings effectively and expeditiously; and manage conflict among individuals in a creative and productive manner.

This approach also aims to develop policies that support teaching improvement. When instructional improvement programs are established, one of the first problems encountered is that policies within the organization do not support such activities entirely. If any of the above programs are to succeed, institutions must have policies that provide positive support for faculty efforts. In the long run, faculty members and other individuals must be assured that they may advance themselves through their efforts. This means that most colleges and universities must make sure their policies—particularly with respect to hiring, promotion, salary, tenure, release time, and leaves—give adequate weight to teaching effectiveness and recognize improvement efforts.

The instructional improvement movement, if successful, potentially could bring fundamental and lasting change to academic life. Specifically, it could lead to faculty placing increasing importance on teaching, a redefinition of faculty workloads to include regular participation in in-service professional development activities, the revision of institutional policies to provide greater support for teaching effectiveness, and the reallocation of resources to finance instructional improvement efforts.

But do we know enough about the complexities of "teaching" and "learning" to improve current practice? Can those who are active in this new area work with faculty colleagues in ways that are both better received and more beneficial than most preservice and in-service programs offered to teachers at the secondary and elementary levels? The answers to these questions are by no means clear at this point. It is too early to expect a rigorous evaluation of faculty, organizational, and instructional development programs. But it is obvious that these programs mark a new era and that they constitute an impressive effort to improve the quality of the educational experience for future students.

10

College for Prisoners

Sylvia G. McCollum

From time to time, newspapers print eye-catching stories about "hardened criminals" who have earned college degrees while locked up in prison. Similarly, magazines run titillating stories titled something like "Rape, Plunder, and Pillage Your Way Through College." The implication, oblique but deliberate, is that if your children are having difficulties getting into college or, if by chance you can't afford their tuition costs, have them break a law and get sent to prison. They will then be on their way to free college educations. These stories, by design or accident, leave the impression that just about everyone in prison takes college courses.

The truth is considerably less spectacular. The prison population in the United States is estimated at approximately 400,000 on any given day. Around 150,000 are either detained in local and county jails or are serving sentences of short duration. A relatively small number, around 23,000, are in federal institutions. The remaining 227,000 are in state prisons.

There are no precise figures of the number of prisoners in the United States currently involved in postsecondary education programs, but it is estimated that the number ranges somewhere between 1 percent and 5 percent, or roughly between a low of 2500 and a possible high of 12,500. Frank Dell'Apa found the figure to be less than 6 percent (around 6400 out of 109,161 prisoners), based on a 60 percent (150 institutions) response to questionnaires sent to 249 adult correctional institutions.[1]

In the federal system in 1974, approximately 2000 prisoners were enrolled in college level courses. Based on an average enrollment of two courses per student, prisoners attended approximately 4000 courses in postsecondary programs. About 550 of these were campus-based classes. The proportion of state prisoners involved in postsecondary education is probably somewhat lower than that in the federal system, except for a few individual states.

It is not known exactly how many students receive associate or bachelor's degrees annually while still incarcerated, but the figure is probably somewhere between 100 and 500 students nationally. It is also difficult to assess the total number of prisoners who could become involved in postsecondary education during imprisonment. Robert Taggert "liberally estimated that there are 30,000 inmates in prisons and jails who could benefit" from access to higher education.[2] Whatever the potential numbers may be, the most immediate problem for educators is establishing access to higher education resources. There are several possible solutions.

One solution can be called precommitment diversion. If the best criminal justice system is one designed to keep people out of prison and uses confinement only as the last resort, then postsecondary institutions should participate in programs that help to divert first offenders from imprisonment. One such program is an experimental demonstration project called Offender Assistance

[1] Frank Dell'Apa, *Educational Programs in Adult Correctional Institutions—A Survey* (Boulder, Colo.: Western Interstate Commission for Higher Education, 1973).
[2] Robert Taggert, *The Prison of Unemployment* (Baltimore: The Johns Hopkins University Press, 1972).

Through Community Colleges. Sponsored by the American Association of Community and Junior Colleges (AACJC) in cooperation with the United States Office of Education Fund for the Improvement of Postsecondary Education (FIPSE), it illustrates what postsecondary education institutions can do at the community level to help keep first offenders out of prison. The idea behind the project was conceived many years ago by R. Frank Mensel, then AACJC vice president. It is now being implemented under the creative and committed leadership of James P. Mahoney. A number of community and junior colleges were invited to submit proposals to describe how they, in cooperation with local criminal justice systems, would provide a continuum of services to first felony offenders to divert them from imprisonment. Three communities—Jacksonville, Florida; Charlotte, North Carolina; and Denver, Colorado—have been selected as demonstration sites. Not all first offender referrals to the program are expected to become college students. Some may get occupational counseling, job development, and placement services. Others may be referred to family counseling, mental health, or other community service centers. The basic purpose of this First Offender Diversion Project is to provide courts and probation services with an alternative to imprisoning offenders so as to avoid the destructive and debilitating impact of incarceration.

Diversion programs are certainly not new. R. T. Nimmer and the American Bar Association Commission on Facilities and Correctional Services have published significant conceptual and descriptive material about such programs.[3] What may be new about this AACJC-FIPSE project is the anticipated precommitment intervention role of *educational* institutions making their resources available to a larger and, in some cases, a new clientele. In addition, it is hoped that the Offender Assistance Project will demonstrate how community and junior colleges can assume a new role—that of establishing appropriate channels between first offenders and other community based resources.

Probably the oldest kind of postsecondary correctional education program is the college course held *inside* a prison. Such courses were offered as early as 1939, predating the first prison

[3] R. T. Nimmer, *Diversion—The Search for Alternative Forms of Prosecution* (Chicago: The American Bar Foundation, 1974).

college survey. A survey published in 1968 found that over half of the existing prison systems offered some form of college program.[4] Approximately 3000, or slightly more than 1 percent, state and federal prisoners, were involved in these programs, practically all of them inside the prisons. A survey three years later estimated that 150 colleges or universities and 121 junior colleges were involved in inmate education.[5] The Newgate Resource Center reported in 1973 that of 305 penal institutions surveyed, 218 (71 percent) offered postsecondary courses. Most of these were offered inside the prisons.

Recent new developments within the higher education community have accelerated the rate at which the number of students involved in college courses inside prisons has increased, such as the University Without Walls and demonstration programs funded by the U.S. Office of Education Teacher Corps. Although portions of these programs take place outside the prison, they are primarily contained within the structure of the correctional institution. Higher education efforts such as the Oklahoma televised instruction system, college-at-home-programs, and others that combine flexible, individualized scheduling and modern technology have also extended the scope of college programs inside prisons.

The logistics of prisoners attending college classes outside the prison are more complicated. Despite substantial success with some study-release programs, their growth rate continues to be very slow. Upward Bound/Newgate efforts that initially began in Oregon, Kentucky, Minnesota, New Mexico, and Pennsylvania combined both inside and outside courses of study, arranged so that the outside portion coincided with the student's approaching release date. As the initial funds provided by the Office of Economic Opportunity ran out and the costs were absorbed by the correctional systems themselves, the outside portions of the programs diminished in duration and importance. However, these programs continue to function, financed either completely by correctional institution budgets or in combination with funds from the Law Enforcement Assistance Administration or the U.S. Office of Education.

[4] S. N. Adams, *College Level Instruction in U. S. Prisons* (School of Criminology, University of California, January 1968).
[5] S. N. Adams and J. J. Connolly, "Role of Junior Colleges in the Prison Community," *Junior College Journal*, March 1971.

A limited number of postsecondary occupational training programs also combine inside and outside classes. In a few cases, vocational technical schools and community colleges near correctional facilities provide *all* the instruction on an outside basis. Prisoner students sometimes participate in the same classes as regular students; in other cases, the prisoners comprise a separate class. Prisoner-student classes take place both during daytime and evening hours, depending on scheduling problems and community and correctional institution understanding and flexibility. In a few instances, prisoner students live on campus either in regular student housing or in separate, supervised half-way houses.

Access to study release or outside college programs—even where minimum security prisoners are serving their sentences in correctional institutions literally surrounded by technical and professional schools, community and junior colleges, four-year colleges, and universities—continues to be minimal and presents a challenging area for educators.

The underlying goal of all prison education efforts is to develop students' interest in continuing their educations, both as a means of staying out of prison and of enriching their personal lives. Most people who work with prisoners can relate impressive anecdotes about individuals who have continued their postsecondary studies after release from prison; except for isolated follow-up studies, however, significant data is not available on the proportion of prisoner college students who attend college after release. We also do not know how many actually receive either an associate or bachelor's degree or a postsecondary technical or professional school certification.

A follow-up study of Newgate students reported a wide variety of problems, conceptual as well as practical, that were inherent in postrelease education pursuits.[6] Continued identification as an offender, lack of emotional as well as financial support systems, overly intensive parole supervision, and time gaps between release and college enrollment are but a few of the roadblocks that require attention if postrelease college programs are to be effective.

[6]Marshall Kaplan, Sheldon P. Gans, and Howard M. Kahn, *An Evaluation of "Newgate" and Other Programs.* Report published by Kaplan, Gans, and Kahn, San Francisco, April 1973. See also, Keith Baker and others, *Summary Report Project Newgate and Other Prison College Programs* (Washington, D.C.: Office of Economic Opportunity, April 1973).

Several areas of concern cut across all prison postsecondary education programs whether they take place inside or outside the institution or on a precommitment or postrelease basis. One of the most critical areas is financing. Prisons that have educational programs generally provide them at no cost to the prisoner up through the high school level. Postsecondary courses, where offered, frequently must be paid for completely, or in part, by the prisoner student. Practices vary by state, ranging from full payment by the student to full payment by the correctional institution. In federal facilities, the situation is similar. Where funds are available and the course of study is an established program goal, all costs are paid by the correctional institution. Otherwise, financing may be shared by institution and student, or the student may pay the whole bill. The institution's budget, the course the student wants, the student's personal financial situation and similar factors help determine what the financial arrangement will be.

An additional cost problem stems from applying out-of-state fee schedules to prisoners who do not reside in the state in which they are incarcerated. The situation is particularly aggravated in federal correctional institutions that house prisoners from many states. Dr. Donald A. Deppe, Education Director of the Bureau of Prisons, recently conducted an informal survey of states in which federal prisons operate. He reported that sixteen states charge in-state resident fees for federal prisoner students and six charge the higher nonresident fees. State and county prisons are faced with a maze of in-county, out-of-county, and related fee schedules. Some colleges have been willing to charge a flat fee ranging from $300 to $750 per inside course, and the prison may enroll as many students in the class as is feasible—generally from 20 to 50. When instructors travel significant distances, mileage fees are an additional cost.

Since most prisoners have limited or no funds, and since their families are similarly situated, cost is a critical issue in making higher education accessible to the offender population. Many prisons still lack sufficient funds to offer adequate literacy, elementary, high school, or vocational training programs. Postsecondary education seems a long way down the road in such instances.

Despite all of the cost problems, the picture is by no means dismal. Some sensitive postsecondary education institutions provide quality education at reasonable prices. Many dedicated instructors travel considerable distances to and from isolated institutions in order to teach one or two hours—sometimes after completing a full teaching schedule elsewhere. In many situations, the readiness of the education establishment to provide services more than equals the readiness of the correctional community to use them.

Financial assistance available from nonprison sources has helped to decrease cost problems somewhat. Prisoner students are generally eligible to apply for educational assistance on the same basis as other students. Veteran's benefits, Basic Education Opportunity Grants (BEOG), federally insured student loans, as well as private group scholarships and grants are increasingly available to prisoner students. In one federal penitentiary I recently visited, twenty-seven of the eighty-seven students enrolled in college level courses were receiving BEOG grants and thirty-three were receiving Veteran's benefits. The Vocational Rehabilitation Administration has been another source of financial assistance when individual students meet the requirements of the vocational rehabilitation program. These education assistance funds are generally available both on an inside and outside basis.

Another critical concern of prison education programs arises from the geographic isolation of some correctional institutions. Despite recent trends to locate new facilities either in or near urban centers, and even though once isolated rural areas are becoming more populated, some correctional institutions are still physically distant from needed resources. In such cases, correspondence courses and various audio-visual programs are alternatives. But initial high student motivation levels are not sustained by correspondence courses and dropout rates continue to be high —both in and out of prison. Closed circuit television and other audio-visual systems can provide college courses in institutions that would otherwise be unable to offer any postsecondary programs, but these efforts are not widespread and operate primarily under experimental conditions.

In addition to the problem of costs and geographic isolation, we can note five additional areas of concern. One is the need to discover ways of strengthening postrelease links between the student and a particular postsecondary institution. Ideally, contact with college admissions staff should be established *before* the prisoner student's release, and specific procedural steps should be taken to insure that the student is enrolled before or very shortly after returning to the community where the receiving education institution is located. Considerable research evidence suggests that the first three months after release from prison are critical. A direct correlation has also been established between the age of released prisoners and the likelihood that they will get into further difficulties. These factors underline the need for prison education efforts to provide early contacts between releasees and structured education situations.

Many prisoners are transferred from one institution to another while serving their sentences, either in the same state or among states in the nationwide federal system. The issue of the transferability of credits is, therefore, another very important concern. Although the College Level Examination Program (CLEP) and other arrangements can help to facilitate the general transferability of earned college credits, transferring credits between education institutions remains a stumbling block. It is a critical issue because it may jeopardize the offender student's involvement in education, particularly if the transfer takes place before a specific course is completed. States that have established separate school districts to provide prison education from kindergarten through grade twelve may want to consider the possibility of extending the school district's responsibility to include postsecondary education. This step alone would not solve all the problems, but at least a framework would exist in which the credit transfer issues might be resolved.

Education, as a program tool, competes with prison industries, institutional maintenance, group therapy, and other demands on available institution program time. Thus, educators must work with correctional administrators to discover ways to schedule classes during daylight hours instead of relegating prison education programs to the evening.

Housing and study space for prisoner students also continue to be problemmatic. A minimum of space and privacy to study and complete education assignments can critically affect whether or not the student will continue in a program. Since most prisoners are housed in institutions designed for containment and punishment rather than programs, it takes a great deal of imagination and good will to provide positive learning environments.

A last major concern is the availability of materials, such as books and mechanical equipment. Some correctional institutions have met these problems creatively by using county or other public mobile library units, interlibrary loan arrangements or by providing time for library work during study-release hours. Special groups such as the Association of American Publishers, Inc., and the American Booksellers Association have donated reference and other books to prisons, but the library situation in prisons remains marginal.[7] A further problem in relation to materials is that the staff of many correctional institutions still view the use of tape recorders and typewriters with suspicion. Members of the education community can make an important contribution by helping such institutions to understand that these machines are needed in the education process, and by helping to supervise their appropriate use.

Prisoner access to educational programs will, in many respects, parallel the access that students in the free world have to similar programs. The major goal, therefore, must be to continue to enlarge postsecondary education opportunities for all potential students.

[7]Marjory LeDonne, *Survey of Library and Information Problems in Correctional Institutions* (Washington, D.C.: U.S. Office of Education, January 1974).

11

Weekend
College

Victor P. Meskill

The *Congressional Record* of November 21, 1966, indicated that Miami-Dade Junior College in Florida enjoyed a "nationwide first" when it began a weekend college in fall 1965. Since then, however, few institutions that have chosen to schedule classes on weekends have experienced the level of response achieved at the C. W. Post Center of Long Island University. This model weekend college began in fall 1971 with twenty-two course offerings and an enrollment of 241 students. Now, with enrollment exceeding 2500 students, the C. W. Post Weekend College offers five degree programs on the undergraduate and graduate level and schedules more than 160 courses per session. Given the current crisis in higher education, one is inclined to ask, "What could account for this most enviable success story?"

One answer to that question would have to be that most, if not all, institutions conducting weekend programs in this country have successfully identified a significant market for weekend study opportunities. C. W. Post was no exception. Potential new learners for a weekend college program include a wide range of people who find it impossible or inconvenient to attend either day or evening classes during the week, such as housewives who lack baby sitters except on weekends; industrial workers, business people, and teachers who are too tired for evening classes; individuals who live too far away for frequent drives to the campus, but are able to manage infrequent trips without undue hardship; people who seek to return to study after a significant time lapse; college graduates who seek personal enrichment or professional growth; and individuals who seek to use their ever-increasing leisure time more productively. In addition to this target group, weekend college provides added options for academically talented high school seniors who wish to enrich their educational experiences or to begin their college studies while still in high school, as well as for those members of the regular college student body who wish to accelerate their degree studies.

The C. W. Post Weekend College was developed with the objective of serving adult students by making higher education available at a time and place most convenient for them. (Incidentally, classes on Saturday and Sunday resulted in a more efficient use of campus facilities.) Communities contain working adults. A simple questionnaire can determine if they are interested in post-secondary education and when they would prefer to attend classes. Time determinations are relatively simple once the target population is identified. The more difficult assignment is to serve the specific educational interests of the community. Perhaps a brief description of the degree programs at this model weekend college will show how their objective was accomplished.

The upper-division Bachelor of Science degree in nursing, which was developed and implemented after extensive needs analysis, allows the registered professional nurse to learn while earning. The practical experience that is necessary in such a program is provided through use of clinical facilities that normally lie dormant on weekends. As most nursing educators know, the scarcity of laboratory facilities is a limiting factor in many of their programs.

The Master of Professional Studies in health care administration is designed to serve the needs of health care personnel who seek to increase their knowledge of managerial and behavioral sciences as applied to their profession. Persons who now hold administrative posts and wish to maintain their certification, or those who want to prepare for administrative posts, find this program particularly beneficial. Students are able to attend classes without interrupting their careers or decreasing their incomes.

The Master of Professional Studies in criminal justice was set up to help students further their careers in such areas as corrections, correctional administration, court administration, law enforcement, probation, parole, and crime and delinquency prevention. One reason the weekend time slot is so suitable for these professional programs is that many of the community's resources —from judges, district attorneys, and hospital administrators to a full range of physical facilities—are more readily available at this time.

Weekend College also offers liberal arts programs. The Associate in Arts in humanistic studies is a response to a desire expressed by industry—that of broadening and deepening the humanistic awareness of business personnel, and thus permitting the college and business community to become more closely involved. The Associate in Arts Degree in General Studies offers adults a "non-declared major," a chance to direct their efforts toward achievable and recognizable academic goals without specifying a particular study area. The general studies program also serves as a stepping stone to other fields the student may wish to pursue at a later date.

In an effort to refine the parameters of Weekend College, all students enrolled in the first session were asked about their educational goals and ambitions. Their responses gave institutional planners an insight into the types of students they were attracting and indicated directions for future academic programs. The institution then contacted the most appropriate professional associations, public agencies, corporations, and organizations to explore their educational needs. This activity resulted in the development of the existing degree programs, and it continues to serve as a basis for developing new programs. As programs are shaped by answering the question of "who's out there?" peer group recruiting activities can be used to continue the thrust. Students in Weekend

College, perhaps more than anyone else, know potential students who could be served by the college. Their efforts in spreading information about the college have contributed a greal deal to the continued growth of the Weekend College.

At first glance, one might conclude that the C. W. Post Weekend College, except for its rapid growth, is typical of other programs and therefore not truly innovative. However, closer inspection reveals that the nontraditional aspect of this program extends beyond the type of student it serves and its unique format. The C. W. Post Weekend College incorporates a complete package that enables the institution to challenge potential learners by saying, in effect, "You just ran out of excuses." In fact, this challenge successfully serves as a lead-in for the college's advertising campaign.

External degree programs, the Empire State College learning contract framework, the University Without Walls, and other open university programs are meaningful approaches to meeting the needs of many of the very same students for whom Weekend College is targeted—primarily adult learners. For a large number of these potential new students, problems other than time and place affect their involvement in higher education. For example, although many potential adult learners are highly motivated, a large number lack the self-discipline to pursue degree studies entirely off-campus or on an independent basis. A corollary to this problem is that adults fear they will fail because they have been removed from formal education for an extended period of time. Such problems can be resolved if institutions of higher education identify learner needs and package existing resources to respond to them. Addressing itself to this situation, Weekend College structure provides a combination of intensive classroom experiences, independent study, and individual consultation with the instructional staff.

The program of Weekend College further recognizes adult learning needs by flexible scheduling. Students can earn up to six academic credits on the undergraduate or graduate level in a period of six or eight weeks. There are three distinct schedules: six hours of instruction for six consecutive Saturdays; six hours of instruction for six consecutive Sundays; or two intensive weekends with eight hours of instruction per day (both Saturday and Sunday) separated by a six-week interval. In any one of these schedules, the student is able to complete a three-credit course of instruction. To supplement the intensive classroom experience, the student is assigned independent study work exceeding that of a traditional class. This approach appears to do much to solve the difficulties of completely independent study.

Other needs of the adult learner are also served by this format. For example, the intensive classroom experience helps develop a greater rapport and a sense of comraderie among the students and faculty, often overcomes the fear of failing, and rapidly develops a sense of personal involvement among all concerned. The imaginative use of lunch periods as an extension of the classroom, an integral part of the program, has the effect of humanizing the entire learning experience. The independent study component assures that material will be covered adequately and encourages the student to learn how to learn; it is a healthy step away from depending on faculty alone for learning achievement. The format of Weekend College also creates an interdependence among the members of the class, for students will often seek out a classmate for assistance and reassurance; they are more likely to do so as a result of the intensive group nature of the classroom experience.

Students, of course, must have access to faculty throughout the program. Specific faculty office hours and available telephone contact times are made known to all participants, for the consultative component is essential to the success of this program. In addition, a specially designed course to develop speed reading and study skills is offered before each Weekend College session to build enrollee self-confidence. The library and other support services are available at times convenient to the student. Special tours are arranged to familiarize the new adult learner with the facilities and operation of the academic support services. Library orientation sessions are held. Printed materials describing class assignments, required texts, and other related information are provided to the student before the first meeting of the class so that the extended class hours can be used most beneficially.

Weekend College still has problems that it must resolve before the institution truly can assert that a potential student has "run out of excuses." A question frequently asked is: "Who is going to take care of my children when I go to school?" The children of Weekend College students are offered the opportunity to enroll in a creative arts learning program at one of Long Island's finest private schools. The curriculum includes music, dance, painting, mixed media, ceramics, architecture, sculpture, and drama. While the parent or parents attend weekend classes, the child is provided with an exciting learning experience.

Another problem still frequently encountered is this one: "The Weekend College is a good idea. However, this is the time I usually spend with my spouse." As an attempt to meet this problem, the C. W. Post Weekend College offers a tuition reduction plan for spouses, thus encouraging husband and wife to study together, rather than to follow the traditional pattern of sending one partner through first, with the second to follow. At Weekend College, therefore, the entire family—husband, wife, and offspring —can take part in an educational venture at the same time.

A major question is financial: "How can I arrange to pay for courses?" Weekend College students may opt to charge their tuition by commercial credit card. They may either pay their charge account immediately, thereby avoiding finance charges, or space their payments out to suit their own budgetary needs. Most adults possess credit cards and are much more familiar with them than with the complicated financial aid forms of most institutions.

Regular full-time college faculty are the primary resource of Weekend College. Through them, the program is integrated into the mainstream of the academic structure, and academic stability is assured. At the same time, the Weekend College learning situation can be constantly compared to the traditional college learning experiences directed by the same faculty. Faculty, students, administrators, and the community all think the Weekend College at C. W. Post is one program worthy of the pride it has generated.

Obviously, the academic integrity of an institution is in no way diminished by linking a formal learning experience (traditional or nontraditional) with a series of nontraditional, nonacademic services. Weekend College is a learner-centered reform at work. Perhaps the magnitude of change reflected by such a program was captured best in a *New York Times* article on November 5, 1973: "When some of the current crop of students at a university branch here look back fondly on their college days, the only two days they'll have in mind are Saturdays and Sundays."

PART THREE

Measure
of Success

There are two ways to view evaluation. One is to think of it as a grim judgment process—a process of approval or disapproval. In this sense, evaluation works like a blade, separating good learners from bad learners, good teachers from bad teachers, good programs from bad programs. The other way to view evaluation is to think of it as a constructive activity that can improve the performance of a program or person by distinguishing relative strengths and weaknesses. Which view one subscribes to may be a function of whether or not one is the object of evaluation. Evaluators themselves, or disinterested observers of the evaluation process, have little difficulty accepting the positive view. The difficulty is convincing those who are being evaluated. For them, the threatening aspects of evaluation look stubbornly real. The persistent dilemma of evaluation might be summed up in the question: "How do you take the sting out without removing the meaning at the same time?"

In the first chapter of Part Three, Harold L. Hodgkinson analyzes evaluation principles as they apply to virtually all phases of academic activity, both traditional and nontraditional. Reporting on a national study of evaluation practices, Hodgkinson offers examples to show that good evaluative criteria are the result of asking the right questions about the activity being evaluated. Standards, on the other hand, tend to be chosen somewhat arbitrarily from among several classical alternatives. A student may be compared to an idealized concept of excellence, to classmates, to earlier classes, or to the student's own level of performance at an earlier stage. But what standards are chosen is probably less important than communicating what those standards are, Hodgkinson feels. Likewise, evaluators should state the purpose of the evaluation process—whether it is to rank students, to weed out the less capable, or to signify a level of competence. By reducing uncertainties about evaluation standards and purposes, evaluators will not only reduce consumer complaints about higher education but they will also reduce the fears that uncertainty generates.

Another way to take the sting out of evaluation is to liberalize grading, which has been a trend in recent years. John G. Bolin considers the impact of liberalized grading on honors. Citing a pilot study that shows the percentage of honors graduates rising from 14.2 in 1964 to 20.8 in 1969 to an amazing 42.2 in 1974, Bolin wonders whether conferring or receiving honors has any meaning at all any more—either to society, the student, or the institution. The time has come, he believes, to either restore the credibility of grades or do away with them altogether in favor of a pass/fail or pass/no-credit system.

The bachelor's degree, one of the most important symbols of learning in our higher education system, is examined by Jonathan R. Warren. The degree has become so vague and varied that its meaning is lost, Warren says. Nevertheless, he does not believe the solution is to abandon degrees or even to subject them to a narrower definition. Instead, he proposes alternative forms of certification to spell out a degree holder's competencies. These alternative forms would supplement the degree, not replace it, and they would serve the needs of both employers and graduate schools.

The remaining chapter of Part Three reports on an evaluation of contract learning at Empire State College. Among the ques-

tions tackled by Timothy Lehmann are: Which kinds of students are drawn to contract learning? Which seem to do best in this approach? And how do students rate their learning experiences at the college? The responses are overwhelmingly favorable to contract learning, but they also pinpoint some of the problems of this approach—for example, how can it be used with learners who have trouble adjusting to independent study? It is fitting that Lehmann's report is developed from individual student evaluations since, in contract learning, students help to determine how they themselves will be evaluated. This increased participation by learners in deciding what constitutes the measure of success is clearly one way to take the sting out of evaluation.

Has the meaning of evaluation been diminished along with the sting? That question, as Bolin and Warren suggest, and as Robert O'Neil suggested at the beginning of this book, still needs answering.

William Ferris

12

Evaluation to Improve Performance

Harold L. Hodgkinson

Innovations in teaching-learning strategies or in delivery systems would seem to call for new ways of formulating student learning outcomes. For the most part, however, they have not prompted such action. With the important exception of innovations geared explicitly to content (for example, programs in the affective domain), student learning outcomes remain much the same in both innovative and traditional programs. This finding was one of several that turned up in a study I recently completed for the Department of Health, Education and Welfare.[1] If one thinks

[1] The final report, titled "Improving and Assessing Performance: Evaluation in Higher Education," is available from the Center for Research and Development in Higher Education, University of California, Berkeley.

about it, the finding is not very surprising. Most innovations fall
into three broad categories: new audiences, new approaches to
teaching-learning, and new delivery systems. They are not designed
to develop new content but to teach existing content better or to
a new clientele. The similarity of student learning outcomes in
traditional and innovative programs allows us to evaluate compara-
tively innovative and traditional programs. Such evaluations are
important because they can help administrators, faculty, students,
funding agencies, and the public find out if the innovations have
been successful. The criteria for evaluation, however, are not and
should not be the same for both types of programs.

The study indicated that new forms of higher education
require new means of assessment, primarily because many innovations use assessment in a new way. Over two hundred institutions
are now using, or are seriously considering adapting, some form of
competency-based education. Because competency-based learning
emphasizes clarity of instructional goals, it increases the importance of evaluation. In-coming students are often diagnosed
(assessed) to see which competencies they may have already
attained and how much work they must do to be certified as competent in the others. Whereas in traditional programs evaluation is
primarily linked to the credentialing process, in competency programs it is also used as a formative teaching tool. In other words,
students are made aware of the criteria and standards for certification in a competency, and their progress is frequently measured so
that help can be provided as necessary. Assessment that simply
places students in a percentile or just discriminates between passing
and failing is not adequate for competency-based programs. Formative diagnostic advice is needed—information that tells if the
student is "real-world" competent.

Contract learning is another innovation that individualizes
the learning process; it too requires individualized assessment.
Many colleges employ a contract with a category called "Procedures for Evaluating Completed Contract." This category requires
that both student and faculty member agree on what will be
regarded as satisfactory work and how that work will be assessed.
Further, most contracts require that evaluations be much more

Appreciation and thanks go to my two colleagues in the project, Julie Hurst
and Howard Levine.

specific than general course work evaluations. Students on contracts are generally interested in a specific problem, and the evaluation should be designed around that problem. Students quite
often produce products—essays, photographs, works of art, poems
—and they expect direct, not proxy, evaluations. Comparing students to one another is almost useless. Since the evaluation must
be specifically designed for each contract, faculty members who
write contracts must be skillful in developing and implementing
evaluation procedures.

Perhaps far more than is realized, individual faculty members in all kinds of institutions are constantly involved in the
processes of evaluation. A partial list of evaluation tasks includes
working on personnel committees (hiring, promotion, tenure);
assessing new course materials (books, audio-visuals, new class
structures); revising courses in the light of past experience and new
materials; and student assessment (diagnosis, course performance,
letters of recommendation).

Faculty members and administrators are also the objects of
evaluation. Their performance is judged in relation to many activities, including grant proposals, research submitted for publication,
the handling of personnel, teaching performance, and program success. Since a large percentage of an individual faculty member's
time is linked with evaluation, it is important to understand the
skills and techniques of good evaluation.

Good evaluation means asking good questions. The primary
question is: What type of judgment is required? Are we looking
for results that would allow us to state a generalization, or are we
interested only in judgments about a certain person, treatment, or
group? Is the goal of the evaluation to factor out certain causes or
do we want to make a blanket judgment about a new system?
Must the judgment relate cost-effectiveness data to educational
data or are we interested simply in educational data? Both the role
of the evaluation and the type of judgment to be made must be
settled before the evaluation is planned and put into practice.

No matter what is being evaluated—student progress, program progress, faculty teaching—those who are evaluated should
know in advance what type of data will be used for the judgments.
Choices must be made from among numerous data possibilities:
student behaviors such as test scores, questionnaire responses,
interviews, and patterns of locomotion; program measures such as

the number of students affected, cost per pupil, and dissemination plan; and teacher effectiveness features such as pre- and post-tests, number of students attracted to the major, teacher-assistant comments, and number and flexibility of office hours. In fact, the evaluator often has the problem of determining which data have the greatest relevance. Which of the almost infinite behaviors, measures, and features are most germane to answering pertinent evaluation questions?

Despite all these possibilities, however, many people new to evaluation face what they regard as a paucity of measurable behaviors and features. The activity to be evaluated appears monolithic and one that cannot be broken down into its component parts. This seeming impasse may have many causes: evaluators may be placing too much emphasis on goals and not enough on the means used to reach the goals; they may believe that understanding, insight, sensibility, and inspiration are immune to public inspection; or they may be uncertain about what questions evaluation should try to answer.

These two problems—too many behaviors, measures, and features, or too few—may be viewed as the paradox of criteria. But if we have asked the right questions, generating criteria to answer those questions should not be difficult. If we wish to know how skilled a student is in statistics, our criteria might include conversance with terms such as *mean, variance,* and *standard deviation,* knowledge of probability calculus, and ability to test for independence. These criteria could be gathered by testing or by checking the student's records for previous exposure to statistics. More complicated skill areas such as personnel management might include criteria that reflect not only cognitive skills but affective skills—for example, the abilities to chair a meeting, to conduct a job interview, or to reduce interpersonal tensions. Measuring performance in relation to these criteria might be accomplished by simulations, unobtrusive measures, and role playing. Regardless of the activity to be evaluated, good criteria can be developed only by asking good questions.

Frequently one good question leads to another. If we want to know whether a program is meeting its objectives, we must know what the program objectives are. We might determine that a major goal of the program is to help people become better decision-makers. This leads to the question, "What competencies can we measure to tell if people are good decision-makers?" Appropriate competencies for good decision-making might include the abilities to discern relevant options, to foresee consequences of actions, and to participate effectively in a decision-making group. Data for measuring these competencies might be collected by using educational games, role playing, student journals, and personal interviews.

Or suppose an objective, such as "filling an educational need," is found to be an amorphous, nebulous one. We must then ask, "What criteria can we use to tell us if the program filled an educational need?" Among the criteria we could use to answer this question are number of students affected by the program, the social significance of the program, and absence of alternatives to that program. These criteria could be collected through questionnaires, a literature search, and progress checks of the program.

If we are unsure of the questions we want the evaluation to answer, we probably will not know which criteria to collect. As a consequence, we might try to collect everything, thinking that we can always decide on appropriate criteria later. There are two serious problems with this approach. First, collecting data is expensive; second, we still will not be able to consolidate the criteria until we determine which questions the evaluation is designed to answer.

It is not always clear which criteria will provide the best evidence. Suppose we wanted to answer the question, "Is Professor Smith a good teacher?" We might decide that criteria such as "stimulates class discussion" and "is democratic in class" would be good evidence of his ability. However, there is no correlation between teaching ability and these criteria.[2] Millions of dollars have been spent in educational research to determine statistical correlations and causal relationships among various educational phenomena. As evaluators, we would do well to search the literature on the content area of the evaluation in order to determine which criteria are reliable indicators and which are not.

In addition to wrestling with criteria, successful evaluators must deal with the problem of educational standards. Unlike the

[2] For a lengthy discussion of research in this field see Robert W. Heath and Mark A. Neilson, *The Myth of Performance-Based Teacher Education*, Report commissioned by the Far West Laboratory for Educational Research, San Francisco, 1973.

clearly functional standards in car manufacturing (if there is an error in the size of a cylinder head, an automobile simply will not run), standards are difficult to determine in education. How much should a student be able to do? At what point? And why? What should be the proper relationship between student performance and credentialing? How many students should complete a program in accordance with individual performance standards before we can say that the program is a success? Too often, the answers to these questions are decided by whim. Many of the consumer-oriented lawsuits filed against colleges and universities arise because standards are alleged to be arbitrary or capricious.

Arbitrariness can happen in a number of ways. The standards may never be clearly articulated; they may not be applied uniformly; or they may be articulated but inherently unfair to certain groups. Students seem increasingly unwilling to allow universities or colleges to use standards that they are unable to defend rationally. An applicant to a professional or graduate school no longer simply accepts the news that he or she has been rejected. The courts, in turn, argue that an educational credential must be job-related if people without the credential are rejected from consideration for that job.

One rationale seems to be that standards, even arbitrary ones, are necessary to control who has access to higher education. For example, during the late 1950s, such a large number of students sought college entrance that the scholastic aptitude examinations were developed to help screen prospective enrollees. The standards were not designed to measure performance directly; rather, they were intended to indicate who had the greatest "promise" and, thus, who should be awarded a scarce resource—a college education. These examinations, as well as high school grades, also were assumed to predict success in adult life. However, studies have shown that grades in college (which presumably are predicted by Scholastic Aptitude Test scores) do not predict success in later life very well at all.

The use of College Level Examination Program tests for advanced placement or credit reflects a similar pattern of arbitrariness. The cutoff points have been adjusted up and down by institutions on the often whimsical basis of how many students the administrators think should pass. If 50 percent of the applicants passed, and the administrators consider that too many, then the required CLEP score might be raised so that only the "proper" number of students, say 25 percent, would pass.

In relation to standards as they are applied by faculty members in the same institution, one finds that there are wide variations. The same performance that rates an A from one instructor may be worth only a C from another. The performance has not varied; what has varied are the standards established by different faculty members. We might well ask: "Where do faculty members get their standards?" The possible answers all involve comparison strategies. First, the faculty member may compare an individual student's score with norms collected from scores of previous students whom he has taught. Second, the individual student's score may be compared with the score of all the students who happen to be taking that course during that particular year. Usually referred to as "grading on the curve," this strategy attempts to develop a normal distribution of student scores and to assign grades based on where students fit into that distribution. Third, the performance of some ideal student may be the basis for an instructor's standards; in such an instance, the faculty member may say, "I know an A when I see one." Unfortunately, one is unable to determine the validity of the standards because the ideal student is a Platonic abstraction.

Most students never know whether they are being compared to all the previous students that the instructor has had, to the Platonic ideal, or to the students who make up one particular class. One could argue that it would be in a student's best interest, and almost his or her right, to know the reference group for the standards. Similarly, a faculty candidate for tenure might not know if he or she were being compared to the "current competition," all previous faculty members, or some unspecified ideal. The matter of three different reference groups also applies to evaluating specific programs. Although the reference could be identified for evaluating students, faculty, or programs, in practice it seldom is.

Standards may also be developed by comparing an individual's performance with his or her own previous performance on tests or on the basis of other criteria. Evaluations over time can help to establish a "sample" of a particular person's behavior; this sample helps to indicate how much development has occurred during the instructional process. Such samples can also be used in programmatic and institutional evaluation. This strategy seeks to obtain a "net gain" of evidence: performance is evaluated "at entry"; it is compared to performance at the end of the time period; and some judgments are made about net gain. Many standards, however, are based only on performance data gathered only at the end of the time period. Formative standards are rarely used. How much is a student expected to learn during the course itself? How much is a faculty member expected to develop during the years of teaching? How much is a new program expected to improve during its first year? Arriving at answers to questions such as these is a complex process because of variations in individual aptitude, ability, and previous learning.

At first glance, it would appear that modules and competency-based programs have little need for certain kinds of standards. No standard assessment in the form of a grade is usually necessary as long as a module is completed. Within competency-based programs, other innovations, and narrative transcripts, however, the question of "how much is competent" is extremely important. Few programs have successfully answered the question. It is not enough to say, "We wish our students to be competent in X." One still needs to ask, "How much of X is needed in order for the student to be deemed competent?" Even modules have levels of attainment (standards) built in.

If one looks at all of the new innovative programs in higher education, as well as the evaluation techniques developed for them, one finds that the question of standards plagues them continually. During the HEW study, we found that contract learning was often very effective in specifying the *criteria* that students were to meet and to some extent the *techniques* whereby the evaluation would be done, but very few contracts specified the level of attainment or *standard* the student was to reach. The same is true of portfolios and narrative transcripts, which give a great deal of information on the criteria for student judgments as well as some techniques, but which lack information on standards. As far as standards are concerned, these new programs seem not much better than the conventional programs they are designed to replace. Just as an A does not mean the same thing as one moves from one faculty member to another, so the judgments of a portfolio or a jury panel may reflect similar inconsistencies. At two schools using jury panels to evaluate student performance, the "easy" juries are fairly well known among students and are being overloaded, while juries known as "tough" are avoided whenever possible.

Accreditation teams have similar difficulties in making decisions on standards. Do all institutions currently accredited form the reference group? Is the reference some ideal notion of what a good institution should be? Or, is it based on the current candidates for accreditation in terms of who are the best and who are the worst? These same questions can be raised about a faculty member who is being considered for tenure, for an academic department or program, or for an administrator or governing board. In all of these cases, the reference group with which the person's performance is being compared is rarely specified. The solution is relatively simple but difficult to implement. The evaluating agency should be required to specify the individual or group with which the person's or program's or institution's performance is being compared. It may sound like a trivial requirement, but if it were set, it would cause a major revolution in the application of higher education standards.

In summary, the four major dimensions of standards clarification are: to specify the individual or group that establishes the standards—whether an external accrediting agency, the faculty member himself, or the institution; to specify the reference group with which one will be compared, as well as the method of comparison; to specify the nature of the standard—whether it is a measure of job performance based on successful "real world" performance in that job, an idealized notion of what a perfect performance should be, or simply an arbitrary number selected from some table of distributions along a standard scale; and to specify the function of the standard—whether it is to reject people and programs, to help them improve their performance, or to admit them to some specialized fraternity, such as an occupational group or a professional school. The individual being evaluated has a right to know these things.

Two types of thinking about evaluation are nearly always unproductive. The first is that evaluation should be an afterthought, something to be tacked on to a project, a course, or an institutional assessment after the activity has ceased. This attitude leads people to think about evaluation as an "add-on" rather than as an "add-in." If I have a grant for $50,000 to develop a programmed text, but have to spend $5000 on evaluation, then I have only $45,000 left to produce the text. This is the wrong attitude. Evaluation should be conceived as an essential part of the production process, just as typing the manuscript would be. Indeed, without effective evaluation, there is a good chance no one will be persuaded to use the text. The price of evaluation may well be $5000, but its value to the project may be far greater than that.

The second type of unproductive thinking involves political considerations. Because most sponsoring agencies like to hear nice things about the projects they fund, they probably would not continue to use an evaluator who always makes negative judgments about programs. Just as tough evaluators run out of clients, so a faculty member who gives mainly C's and D's may well run out of students. Politics and the law of supply and demand do relate. Nonetheless, the political impact of evaluation can be minimized if the reason for the evaluation, the standards to be expected, and the credibility of the evaluation process and the evaluator are clearly established.

If the issues surrounding evaluation were confronted squarely, students might well be happier about their educational experience, faculty and programs might be better understood, and the society might have slightly greater faith in its institutions of higher education.

13

Evaluating Contract
Learning

Timothy Lehmann

During winter 1974, the Office of Research and Evaluation at Empire State College, as part of the Institutional Self-
Study for accreditation, administered a comprehensive Student
Experience Questionnaire (SEQ) to a random sample of students. [1]
Four hundred and eighty-three students, representing 27 percent
of the total student enrollment at the time, returned usable questionnaires.

The questionnaires revealed that Empire State College stu-

[1]This chapter reports on Developing Cost Effective Models for Postsecondary Education, a project partially funded by the Fund for the Improvement of Postsecondary Education, Ernest G. Palola, project director.

dents were different from the typical college student in most demographic dimensions. The average age was thirty-seven years, ranging from nineteen to sixty-eight. Only 10 percent were in the traditional college age group of twenty-two and younger; almost 60 percent were between ages thirty and fifty-five. A striking feature of the ESC age distribution was the fairly even spread among adults from age twenty-three to age fifty-eight. In the SEQ sample, 63 percent was married, 27 percent single, and 9 percent widowed, divorced, or separated. Slightly more than 50 percent were women but only 9 percent were housewives. Students working full-time represented 60 percent of the sample, whereas those working part-time represented 10 percent. One-third of these people were employed in professional and semiprofessional jobs; one-fifth were employed in skilled, semi-skilled, and unskilled jobs; and another one-sixth held middle-level supervisory jobs. Few respondents classified their occupation as student and even fewer reported that they were unemployed. Only 7 percent described their present occupation as unsatisfying, as compared to 64 percent who described it as rewarding.

Almost 80 percent of Empire's students had prior college experience; 29 percent had associate degrees and 8 percent had graduate level training or a degree upon admission. Students with only a high school diploma or less formal education represented 8 percent of the sample; another 4 percent had been to a trade school. When asked why they enrolled at ESC, students cited three main reasons: receiving credit for prior learning (35 percent), the independence allowed by the college (30 percent), and flexibility (21 percent). For Empire students, flexibility means not only a lack of formal requirements (such as class attendance) but—more importantly—the chance to work and study simultaneously. When asked to rank their reasons for going to college, students mentioned three reasons most frequently: academic preparation for graduate school (30 percent); vocational advancement (29 percent); and to satisfy personal desires for a college education and to increase the ability for self-directed learning (20 percent). More traditional liberal arts objectives, such as increasing appreciation for art, were a distant fourth (11 percent).

Based on the SEQ, then, we come up with this picture of Empire students: they are likely to be married, older, working adults who are reasonably content with their present occupation.

They have substantial previous college experience and are attracted by the flexibility of the college, its philosophy, and the opportunities for independent study. As a group, the students are highly motivated, practical in orientation, and have strong vocational and career reasons for pursuing a college degree. As of 1974, it appears that Empire is less attractive to the very young, the very old, minorities, the unemployed, the occupationally disenchanted, or those individuals with a high school or trade school background.

Before we consider other findings of the study, it might be useful to summarize briefly how contract learning works. Each student prepares a degree program statement which brings together personal goals and needs with the educational objectives and program of the college. The degree program is a comprehensive study plan that provides the framework for assessing prior learning and setting up individual learning contracts. Once prior learning is assessed, the remainder of a student's degree program is fulfilled through a series of learning contracts.

As a plan for learning developed jointly by student and mentor, the learning contract has four parts: the general purposes that underlie the student's work; the specific purposes that the contract aims to serve; the learning activities and resources that the student will undertake; and the basis for evaluating the work completed. The contract describes the rights and responsibilities of both student and mentor for a designated period of time within the student's overall degree program. A contract may be either full-time or half-time. A full-time contract normally assumes that the student will study thirty-six to forty hours a week; a half-time contract represents half that number of study hours. The length of the contract is determined by the student's degree plan, but usually the contract runs from one month to six months. Academic credit awarded for contracts is stated in terms of contract months. By definition, a contract month is four weeks.

Contracts are tailored to individual goals, needs, and capacities. They build on the student's background and can take advantage of community resources the student already has identified. Students can move at their own pace, setting the work load and length of the contract in terms of the overall demands on their time. Finally, students participate in determining how the contract work will be evaluated and how this relates to their personal objectives. Learning contracts are intended to allow a great deal of flexibility and individuality in approaching college learning. To what extent does this individualization of learning occur? Can we sort out different kinds of learning contracts and identify different kinds of learning experiences students have? Are some students' contracts more highly structured by the mentor because the student is not ready for such independent study?

In analyzing student influence on contract preparation, we found that students vary considerably in the degree of independence they exhibit. One-fifth of the students were easily classified as very independent in making decisions about their contract learning. These students said they selected the contract topics, selected almost all the learning resources used, selected the evaluation strategy to be followed, and actually wrote first and subsequent drafts of the contract. At the other end of the continuum, 26 percent of the students reported that their mentors were the ones who structured the ingredients of the contract. These more dependent learners allowed their mentors to shape both the academic content and the evaluation procedures. Between the independent and dependent groups, 46 percent reported working jointly with their mentor in setting up contracts.

Another question addressed the student's perception of the mentor role during the contract. Although the pattern of response was similar to the preceding question, the highly dependent student role was less frequent. Only 7 percent of the students indicated that their mentor acted as a tutor, presenting his knowledge on the subject and assigning readings to be mastered as in a traditional college. On the other hand, almost one-third stated that the mentor served as a resource facilitator, giving the student responsibility for contract activities and assisting where needed. Both the student and the mentor worked together on contract activities in 53 percent of the cases.

In contrast to the more dependent learners, the independent learners rated the contract method as superior to traditional methods, rated the learning contracts as more valuable than college courses for personal development, and perceived their mentors as more approachable than faculty at other institutions. Independent learners experienced feelings of confidence and competency, of being challenged to do their best thinking, of finding the connections of life and learning exciting, and of obtaining learning resources when needed. On the other hand, dependent learners were more likely to feel bored and disinterested, to worry about mentor evaluation, to be confused about what they were doing, to be worried and tense, and to use learning resources that opened up new worlds to them. Although the "worried and tense" item was not statistically significant, a slightly higher percent of dependent learners reported being worried than did independent learners. In relation to "learning resources that opened up new worlds," the item may be explained, in part, by the fact that dependent learners relied on their mentors to suggest learning resources appropriate to their interests. With this possible exception, all the experience items regarding contract learning fall into expected patterns —the positive items associated with the independent learners and the negative items with the dependent learners.

A tentative conclusion can be drawn here. The independent learners seemed to be more willing to explore knowledge external to themselves (openness to new ideas, understanding other cultures and people), especially when this knowledge is not gained through direct personal contact. Neither independent nor dependent learners reported that the college influenced them in the area of direct personal interaction. It may be that independent learners were already competent in interpersonal skills at entry and did not see the college as having a major impact here.

One of the most surprising findings of this analysis was that no particular learning resources were associated with the independent learners. Since data about a wide variety of learning resources were collected from the students, we expected to see different patterns for different kinds of students. It would appear that behavioral indicators of this type do not vary significantly with the degree of independence.

Student-mentor interaction is at the heart of contract learning, but the nature and degree of interaction can vary considerably. Although students met with their mentors on an average of once every two weeks, more than one-quarter met with them once a week or more often, whereas one-fifth met monthly or less often. Most students felt that their mentors welcomed contact; only 6 percent reported their mentors "occasionally appeared not interested in their work." The distribution of contacts showed that mentors were available to meet particular student needs as they arose, and that mentors welcomed such contacts when they occurred.

What do students and mentors talk about during these meetings? For most students, the bulk of the time was spent on the content, planning, and evaluation of contracts, with considerable attention also paid to use of learning resources and the student's future plans. Three out of ten students reported they spent a great deal of time discussing topics in the mentor's field of interest. Few students spent contract time on bothersome administrative problems such as scheduling or billing, or on problems from their personal lives. For the most part, students and mentors focused on academic matters and pursued them during the contract periods.

Students were asked how they felt about their contract experiences. Relatively few students stated they were frequently worried (10 percent), bored (4 percent), confused (7 percent), or concerned about mentor evaluation of their work (13 percent). On the other hand, most students said they were frequently interested (87 percent), challenged to do their best thinking (79 percent), confident (73 percent), and found the connections of life and learning exciting (81 percent). In addition, students indicated learning resources were available when needed (75 percent) and opened up new worlds of learning (62 percent). Only a small minority of students experienced anxiety and difficulty during their contracts. Most found their contract activities a challenging, exciting, stimulating learning experience.

One of the most attractive features of Empire State College is the wide array of learning activities and resources that may be used in contracts. Learning contracts may involve independent study under the guidance of a mentor or tutor, attending a formal course at another college, working with an ESC module, or taking a correspondence or a media course. The student may become an intern in a government or social agency, elect to work on a cooperative project with fellow students, or travel abroad with a specific study plan in mind.

Six out of every ten students reported that field experiences were an important part of their contract activities. Field work experience covered such activities as present work experience (49 percent), volunteer social service (20 percent), visits to community agencies (16 percent), and observation of community activities (20 percent). Logs or journals of contract learnings were kept by 60 percent of the students. The primary purposes of the logs were to record learning experiences (60 percent) and to reflect on them (31 percent). Tutors were used in half the contracts and served as specialists in the subject (53 percent), for guidance in content areas (31 percent), or to discuss ideas (12 percent). Very few students reported that they used tutors for remedial work (4 percent).

About one-third of the contracts included some group study (in which students with similar contracts work together) and use of local libraries; one-quarter of the students reported using periodicals and ESC modules. Of the students who used modules, 40 percent found them a helpful guide, 32 percent generally excellent, 9 percent useful in parts, and 7 percent generally stimulating. About 17 percent, however, found modules vague, confusing, or simply not very helpful. One out of every six students took courses at other colleges in the state. Another 10 percent took advantage of SUNY independent study courses, and over 70 percent of these students found them to be helpful. A wide variety of other learning resources were used in student contracts. It is clear from the data reviewed here that the students were taking advantage of community and other learning resources.

One series of questions in the SEQ asked the students to evaluate the contract method in terms of its strengths and weaknesses and to compare it to more traditional classroom methods. Since most of the students had two or three years of previous college work in traditional settings, and since some were taking college courses as part of their contract work, the students were in a unique position to compare traditional and nontraditional methods. Almost 50 percent of the students rated the learning contract method as very superior to traditional methods of learning; 27 percent said it was somewhat better; 15 percent said the two methods were comparable; and, only 3 percent found the contract method inferior to classroom instruction.

When students were asked to compare the learning contract method with the traditional method in relation to their personal development, 60 percent checked "much more valuable than a regular college course," 14 percent said "a little more valuable" and another 14 percent indicated "about the same as previous course work." Again, only 3 percent found the contract method less valuable than traditional methods. On the basis of these two questions, three-quarters of Empire State's students rated the learning contract method superior to traditional methods.

The two strengths most identified by the students were flexibility (51 percent) and the opportunity for self-directed learning (39 percent). The contract process helped 16 percent of the students clarify their educational goals, and another 12 percent appreciated the noncompetitive aspects of contract learning. Nine out of ten students did not mention weaknesses in the learning contract process. A small minority of students did indicate that more group exchanges were needed (12 percent), that the required self-discipline and motivation was too difficult (10 percent), and that writing contracts to ESC standards and evaluating work completed was too hard (9 percent). The following were identified as weaknesses by 7 percent of the students: difficulty in allocating the right amount of time to contract work; difficulty in amending contracts to explore other interests; and difficulty in locating books and tutors. Another small group of students (6 percent) stated that the contract method relies too much on a single mentor for planning, guidance, and instruction. Those who cited these weaknesses may not have been well prepared for independent study and may have needed more structure in their learning experiences at the beginning of their ESC work. Overall, contract learning at ESC appeared well designed to meet the needs of most students.

Empire State College has a set of educational objectives and competencies that should be met by all students at some point in their degree program. Some students may have developed these competencies before entering Empire; other students focus on particular objectives during one or more of their contracts. These educational objectives are broken down into two major groupings—cognitive and affective. In the Student Experience Questionnaire, we included these objectives as outcomes that the students could evaluate as part of their contract learning. For example, we took the conceptual outcome, "ability at analysis," and defined it as the ability to break down a communication or experience into its basic elements and to make explicit the relationships among them. The ability to recognize unstated assumptions, the skill to distinguish facts from hypotheses, and the ability to detect logical fallacies in an author's argument are examples of analysis competencies. Each student was asked to rate how much contract time was spent in analysis activities on a four-point scale from "very little" to "almost all the time." We followed a similar process for every outcome used in the survey.

When we examined the cognitive outcomes, we found that students spent a great deal or almost all their time on analysis and synthesis, somewhat less time on evaluation and application, and relatively little time on memorization. The low memorization rate may mean that factual knowledge and concepts are not emphasized enough in fields requiring substantial knowledge bases for advanced work. On the other hand, the college stresses competence in higher order cognitive processes and the data show students spending their contract time developing these skills. It seems that mentors have found ways to get students engaged in complex mental activities.

Two additional cognitive outcome items were evaluated by students. Over three-quarters of the students said that they increased their intellectual competence and curiosity (to a moderate or major extent) as a result of their contract learning. A large number of students (64 percent) also reported that they increased their job related competencies. These responses to contract questions fit rather well with the reasons students gave for enrollment at ESC. It appears that the practical interests of students and the more intellectual and developmental interests of mentors blend well in the contract format of ESC experience.

One of the special features of ESC is that it gives a great deal of weight to objectives in the affective domain. As a result of studying at the college, students are expected to become increasingly aware of social relationships, to refine and clarify their purposes, to become more independent, to improve their understanding of themselves and others, and to work effectively with others. How well are students achieving these objectives? About two-thirds reported that the college, to a moderate or major extent, had influenced their competencies in increasing awareness, self-understanding, and self-reliance. About six out of every ten students indicated that clarifying purposes and self-consistency were realized to a moderate or major extent. Interpersonal competence and understanding others were the affective outcomes showing the least impact from contract learning. The college's emphasis upon independent study, and the corresponding lack of contact students have with each other, may make it more difficult for students to achieve substantial gains on these objectives.

Asked to evaluate the quality of their learning experiences, 41 percent of the students stated that they were more than adequate, another 46 percent found them adequate, and only 7 percent indicated insufficient quality; 2 percent reported that assessing quality was not part of their ESC experiences. In terms of the general level of satisfaction with educational experiences at the college, students were very well (63 percent), or fairly well (30 percent), satisfied. Only 5 percent indicated they were not satisfied; 2 percent did not answer the question. On these general satisfaction items, the college appears to have met student needs and expectations for their degree programs successfully.

Several implications for other colleges may be drawn from the data presented on contract learning in this paper. First, contract learning seems particularly well suited to a certain type of student. For older, working, married adults who may have already attended several colleges, contract learning provides both the structure and flexibility they need. Often carrying a heavy work load, as well as family and community responsibilities, these students are generally highly motivated to obtain degrees. They need an educational setting outside the constraints of the typical classroom and campus. They need access to education that fits their busy daily schedule, that allows them to proceed independently at their own pace, and that provides a challenging evaluation of the learning that occurs. The contract-mentor system fits these learning conditions well.

Second, our findings indicate that at entry and throughout the degree program, students differ in their ability to handle independent study. Students identified as the more independent learners clearly evaluated their contract experiences much more favorably than did dependent learners. They also reported that the college had a moderate or major impact on their attaining cognitive and affective competencies. On the other hand, those students who are younger, or who lack clearly specified goals, may need more structured learning conditions during their initial contracts in order to achieve such competencies; they require sensitive mentors who can provide appropriate educational supports.

Third, mentors must be able to work effectively with a variety of dependent and independent students. The role of the mentor is crucial if the college is to foster self-directed learning. An experienced, resourceful, and mature group of faculty committed to the ideal of independent learning is needed to support and challenge students having different learning styles. For students initially requiring a more structured faculty response, mentors must be available and willing to put in extra time. They must have the patience necessary to create the conditions whereby the students will accept greater responsibility for their own learning. The major graduate universities today do not prepare teachers for this role; rather, they emphasize disciplinary specialization and research-oriented activities. Recruiting resourceful faculty attuned to contract learning may be an arduous and time-consuming task. Further, research data on ESC mentors consistently show that they would prefer more professional development time during their normal work week. Colleges adopting the contract learning method must be prepared to support and reward faculty in ways that are very different from those of a traditional setting.

Finally, the contracting process itself has substantial educational benefits apart from the subject matter the contract addresses. The very act of negotiating a contract between a student and a mentor may be a valuable learning experience. By raising questions about a student's goals, life plans, the specific objectives for a particular learning contract, the kinds of learning activities and resources to be used, and the ways in which the learning will be evaluated, the dialogue with a mentor stimulates the student to think seriously about his or her education. Students can learn to think maturely about their own development and about the relevance of a particular learning activity in relation to that development. They can take direct personal responsibility for their learning and for gaining skills in self-direction. By thinking carefully about the topics to be learned, by searching out learning activities and resources beyond the campus, and by gaining experience in self-assessment, students prepare themselves for life-long learning. Although many colleges profess that life-long learning is one of their central educational objectives, they often lack a framework that structures actual learning toward this goal. Contract learning is one method that may encourage learning long after a degree is achieved.

14

Alternatives to Degrees

Jonathan R. Warren

Current discussions of higher education are full of catch phrases, including *alternative paths* and *nontraditional education*. Adherents of such programs are accused of lowering standards and cheapening degrees—two more catch phrases. The response to these accusations is that new programs are opening up higher education by making it more responsive to the needs of today's students, or today's world, or some equally ambiguous set of needs. None of these phrases is any more informative than Madison Avenue advertising language, largely because no accepted overall goal for a college education exists. The educational substance for which a college degree stands is undefined.

The motives of people who use the catch phrases are sound.

They are trying to bring enough flexibility and diversity into programs of higher education to make them more serviceable both for their usual clientele and for the growing numbers of older students, part-time students, women, and members of racial and ethnic minorities who are changing the character of the college student population. New categories of students, as well as the newly acknowledged diversity in conventional students, have led to program modifications. Curricula have been revised, academic calendars have been changed, residency requirements have been eased, new opportunities for entering college with advanced standing have been provided, and new pedagogy has been introduced with television, self-paced learning, and off-campus practical experiences. But even with all of this activity, the bachelor's degree stands as it did more than three hundred years ago; it is the undefined and unchanged symbol of the completion of a college education. The present confusion over standards, awarding credit, and accrediting nontraditional programs is hardly surprising since no one is able to describe the common goal toward which they are all directed—the degree.

Nontraditional programs still have the traditional goal of degree attainment. They may clearly state worthwhile and sensible academic objectives that can be reached through means other than the usual classroom activities and that may lead to academic competence similar to that produced by traditional college programs. But when awarding a degree rather than some other recognition of accomplishment terminates the nontraditional program, the implication is that graduates have acquired academic competencies somewhat equivalent to those acquired from traditional programs. Many of the nontraditional programs have carefully defined objectives and can describe accurately what a student may expect to accomplish by completing that program. Yet nontraditional programs cannot be sold only on the basis of clear, worthwhile objectives effectively achieved. They must have the degree attached as the symbol of completion even though what the degree symbolizes —in a more general sense than simply the completion of a particular program—is completely undefined. Of course, traditional colleges do not define the degree symbol either, but that poses little problem because no one asks them what it means.

Accrediting associations might be expected to define what a degree should represent, but the voluntary regional accrediting associations leave the individual institutions free to define their own purposes. Accreditation is to assure only that the institution accomplishes its self-defined purposes. Some purposes, of course, are not considered appropriate for degree-granting programs. However, the criteria for appropriate goals, as set up by state governments that control degree-granting privileges, are vague at best. The accrediting associations try to maintain academic standards by observing the credentials of the faculty, the institution's financial strength, its physical facilities, and its administrative organization. The standards the accrediting commissions maintain are thought to have some bearing on the ability of the institution to produce the academic outcomes that awarding a degree symbolizes, and they probably do. But until the degree and the capabilities it is expected to represent are defined, no one will be able to say whether or not the accreditation process is maintaining the right standards.

The charge that no one knows what a college education consists of or what a degree represents does not mean that individual faculty members are unsure of their goals or that academic departments do not have coherent study programs that bring students to some well defined competencies. Most faculty members expect very specific accomplishments of students taking their courses. At this level of specificity, the purposes of higher education can be well defined, and it may be possible to use them as the foundation for broader purposes.

In relation to departmental objectives, purposes may or may not be well defined. But even carefully formulated departmental objectives cannot replace overall institutional goals. A student takes fewer than half of his or her courses in a particular field in order to satisfy the requirements for a degree. The rest of a student's program typically has so little coherence that no useful definition can be attached to the degree once it is achieved. An occasional exception exists, as at Alverno College in Milwaukee, where the academic requirements for graduation are stated in sufficient breadth and detail to describe clearly what graduates can be assumed to have learned. Unfortunately, it will not be possible to compare degrees from Alverno with those from other institutions until all institutions define what they mean by their degrees.

In the educational process—from individual courses where purpose is usually quite clear, through programs within departments to departments as a whole, and finally to the institutional level where degrees are awarded—the importance attached to clear goals is inversely related to the importance attached to accomplishment. Almost no importance is attached to a student's completion of a few courses, even though half a dozen well selected and integrated courses may represent a significant academic accomplishment that may be associated with a clearly stated educational goal. Further, completion of all the courses needed to satisfy the subject matter requirements for a degree, such as a full program of mathematics courses, is given only moderately greater importance. Not until the student has also completed the remaining hodgepodge of courses required for a degree is the most important and most poorly defined goal, the degree itself, reached.

The importance of the degree is indicated by the use of attrition or completion rates to judge the success of an institution, and by the use of a bachelor's degree, regardless of field, as the prerequisite for employment. Economists use the number of degrees awarded as an indicator of educational productivity. Relatively high attrition rates have been cited as indicators that certain programs, such as the open admissions program at the City University of New York, are not effective. A physics student with a degree can qualify in many states and counties to be a probation officer, while a student who withdrew from college short of a degree cannot—even though his or her major might have been sociology, social psychology, or criminology. The capabilities that would merit the importance given to a degree are not defined. But just because the intrinsic significance of a bachelor's degree is not defined does not mean it does not exist. Proponents of liberal education have argued effectively for the kind of education a bachelor's degree is often intended to represent. Yet practice and educational philosophy have not coincided.

A sensible way out of the confusion would be to relieve the present degree of much of its burden. In some circumstances, employers are prevented by law from using qualifications as poorly specified as those associated with bachelor's degrees as conditions of employment. Even when certain qualifications are not expressly prohibited as job prerequisites, there is little to recommend their use. Employers would do well to specify desired competencies that an academic institution might certify without reference to a degree. That community colleges already offer certification for specific competencies indicates the feasibility of such a procedure. However, four-year colleges may be disinclined to adopt the practice out of fear of losing prestige. Undeniably, the issue is complex. But the importance of granting specific certifications seems great enough to outweigh concerns about academic status.

Academic standards are set largely by individual faculty members, and much of the current uncertainty about those standards is due to the absence of overall purpose. Whereas the standard for one course may be for students to learn enough so that they can go on to a more advanced course, other courses may have no such specific objective. In such cases, standards often become idiosyncratic, variable, and difficult to defend. Yet faculty members usually know what they can expect their students to accomplish and what standards are appropriate for what purposes.

Rather than one alternative path to earning a degree, higher education might do well to offer a variety of alternatives. Alternatives need not be occupational credentials such as those produced by community colleges. A variety of academic capabilities with occupational value could be certified independently of a degree without necessarily making the certificate an occupational one. Competencies in linear algebra, group dynamics, historical analysis, or other academic areas—certified as they were acquired —would at times have occupational value. The competences can be made specific enough to define their applicability without reference to occupational titles.

An ongoing study of the academic capabilities typically associated with bachelor's degrees points up the wide variability in the content of degree programs even in one field and the nature of some of the competencies that could usefully be certified short of a degree.[1] The transcripts of groups of fifty recent graduates in nine fields of study from a variety of institutions showed three or four different patterns of in-field courses; the out-of-field courses showed three or four additional patterns. In-field and out-of-field patterns combined in numerous ways. Since it makes little sense to

[1] The study, directed by the author, is being conducted by Western College Association and Educational Testing Service under a grant from the Fund for the Improvement of Postsecondary Education. The study is scheduled for completion in December 1975.

treat these combinations similarly, let us examine the various components that make up the different patterns.

The transcripts from one institution tended to be similar, although occasionally a transcript was more like those from other institutions. Even in chemistry, where the curriculum is fairly standard across most institutions, this similarity by institution was most common. Transcripts showing similar course patterns could be grouped into clusters that identified three or four types of programs in each field. In history, for example, the geographic area studied was one basis for a broad grouping; in other words, some transcripts showed that 15 to 20 percent of the history courses were devoted to Asian history, whereas others showed little or no Asian history. Almost all the history transcripts showed substantial amounts of American and European history, but the relative proportions differed, providing another basis for clustering. One cluster showed twice as much American as European history; another showed slightly more European than American. One type of transcript differed from others by indicating a heavier emphasis on historiography and the philosophy of historical study. Another cluster, identified by much less depth and scope of historical study than the others, showed a heavy concentration of courses in education in the out-of-field courses. To some extent, prospective public school history teachers take different patterns of courses than do other history majors. Those students whose transcripts showed a heavy emphasis on historiography may have been anticipating graduate study in history.

The clusters of transcripts with similar course patterns were less sharply defined in the out-of-field courses than in the in-field courses. Yet some clear out-of-field patterns emerged. History showed a large cluster of programs in education, for example, while chemistry did not. Other out-of-field patterns—for example in art, music, economics, history, and literature—appeared in several disciplines each. Yet the concept of minors, or secondary majors, did not seem widespread. Instead, it appears that students followed individual interests in selecting courses; although the courses may have complemented each other, they did not necessarily constitute a minor. In most of the fields, one cluster of transcripts could be identified in which the out-of-field courses were so scattered that no more than one course appeared in any field other than the major.

In each of the nine fields, a number of common course patterns appeared that indicated that certain fields were studied in enough depth to warrant recognition. If learning in specific fields were to be recognized as standard practice, the inflated importance of the degree and the confusion caused by attempts to tie programs, academic standards, and employment to it might be reduced.

Despite criticisms of the degree, it should not and need not be abandoned. With other forms of recognition available to serve the selection purposes of employers and graduate schools, it would continue to indicate that a student had completed a study program in the liberal arts or in any coherent aggregate of studies approximately comparable to current four-year programs of study. The long history of the degree is not sufficient reason in itself to continue its use, but it does have value as a familiar and recognized social institution. For it to continue to be a useful indicator of an extensive collegiate education, however, educators must specify more precisely what criteria it represents.

15

Honors
Inflation

John G. Bolin

Many colleges and universities have begun to look with more than passing interest at the growing numbers of students graduating with honors. The roll call for students receiving their bachelor's degrees cum laude, magna cum laude, or summa cum laude seems to be much longer than it was just a few years ago. In the mid-1950s, graduating with honors signified truly outstanding scholarship. Since the early 1960s, however, the significance of a degree conferred with honors has continually declined. At many universities, special notice is no longer given the honors graduate. In fact, honors seem to be taken more or less for granted today. Cum laude tacked onto the end of a name in the commencement program attracts little attention.

144

Precisely how widespread the inflation of honors has become is not known. Although some institutions have made studies of their own grading patterns, few data have been gathered across institutional boundaries to give a basis for a broad assessment of the problem. To gain an initial idea of how figures compared, the honors programs of four major institutions in the Northeast were studied. The percentages of honors degrees conferred in 1964, 1969, and 1974 were analyzed to determine trends. With some variation among the four institutions, the overall trend was significant increases in both the number and percentage of students graduated cum laude or better. In 1964, the percentage of honors graduates at all the institutions was 14.2 percent. By 1969, that percentage had risen to 20.8 percent, and by 1974 it had spiraled to a lofty 42.2 percent.

In addition, the percentage of honors degrees conferred at each level rose, and these growth rates were disproportionate. While the increase in cum laude recipients far outran the increases at the other two levels of distinction on the basis of simple percentages, the proportionate increase of cum laude graduates was far less than that of the other two classifications. Cum laude degrees, for example, increased about two and a half times (255 percent) between 1964 and 1974, whereas the increase in magna cum laude degrees was more than threefold (358 percent), and the rise in summa cum laude degrees was almost fivefold (489 percent).

The significance of this trend is clear. The nature of and perhaps even the philosophy underlying honors in higher education are in the process of change. Moreover, the relative importance of honors has been eroded by the tremendous inflation in the number and percentage of honors graduates. To be distinguished by being recognized as one out of one hundred or one out of twenty-five or even one out of ten has some distinction. When the chances of being so recognized approach even odds, the value attached must be decidedly lessened.

Although the trend is quite clear, the reasons for it are not. Several hypotheses have been advanced. The first and most common in some academic circles is that students of the late sixties and seventies are more academically able and more intelligent than their predecessors. To test this hypothesis, scores that students in the observed classes at each institution in the sample achieved on the Scholastic Aptitude Test (SAT) were compared with the trends in the number of honors conferred. This comparison indicated a strong relationship between honors and SAT scores between 1964 and 1969, but that relationship disappeared between 1969 and 1974. (In contrast, although SAT scores at the sample institutions tended to rise in the latter half of the 1960s, the national mean remained fairly constant. And, during the period from 1969 to 1974, the sample mean stabilized while the national mean declined 2.6 percent.) Honors conferred rose 6.6 percent between 1964 and 1969, while the weighted mean SAT scores for the sample were up 8.2 percent. However, in the next five-year period, the SAT scores remained constant while conferred honors climbed another 21.4 percent. This latter trend quickly dispels the "superior student" theory. Additionally, it has been discovered that students in the public schools seem to be regressing in achievement in advanced mathematics. These would hardly seem to be signs of increasing intellectual ability.

The next hypothesis suggests that the academic requirements for earning honors changed radically during the ten years covered by the study. A review of the standards at each institution for the years in question indicated that this hypothesis, too, could be eliminated. According to institutional representatives, there could have been minor changes in regulations relating to major areas of study—for example, the number of courses in a major area that had to be taken to qualify for honors—however, they knew of no major alterations that would have precipitated the increases indicated by the data.

The third hypothesis deals with the currently popular movement toward pass-fail or pass-no credit grading. In this area, we can see some effect on honors at graduation. Sidney Claunch has developed a probabilistic model that illustrates the inflationary influence that pass-fail courses can have on a student's quality-point average.[1] And Robert Feldmesser notes that when pass-fail courses are offered, faculty members tend to become rather lax about grading students.[2] Thus, increasing the pass-fail and pass-no credit options may result in devaluation of cum laude.

[1] Sidney J. Claunch, "Effects of Pass-Fail Grading on Quality Point Averages," *College and University*, 1972, *47*(2), 93-105.
[2] Robert A. Feldmesser, "The Positive Functions of Grades," *Educational Record*, 1972, *53*(1), 66-72.

A fourth hypothesis, which is to some extent tied to the third, suggests that relative standards of scholarly achievement have declined since the mid-1960s. This charge is extremely difficult if not impossible to prove. Nevertheless, Warren Bryan Martin suggests that the pressure to maintain or to expand college enrollments, to keep students in college and to fill empty spaces, may have caused some colleges to relax academic standards. "In more *avant-garde* colleges," he points out, "it is not uncommon to find that only about 2 percent of the grades assigned are in the D or F categories."[3] Although many colleges would argue that their admissions selection process screens out weaker students, it is highly unlikely that the process is operating at a 98 percent level of effectiveness. Far more likely, faculty expectations for student achievement have changed. Faculty members are simply less concerned about the evaluation of student achievement. In the college classroom today a student may be awarded a C just for attendance; if he does any work at all, he may get a B or an A. Often professors excuse themselves from honest appraisal of their students on the basis that grading interferes with the learning process or that they do not want to be held responsible for "ruining" someone's future career by giving him a poor mark.[4] Many sincere and dedicated faculty members, in fact, question the whole concept of evaluation. They are quick to point out that techniques, as well as evaluative measurements, are often primitive and arbitrary and may be applied erroneously or inconsistently. There is also the argument about the predictive validity of grades—everyone knows that academic success has no relationship to postacademic success.

Unfortunately these attitudes do little to help the student or society. Current grading practices reveal absolutely nothing about a student's interest or ability, nor do they provide any indication of his level of achievement or dedication to learning. Moreover, such practices may well mislead a student who is trying to establish meaningful goals. The purpose of grading is not to predict how well a person will do on the job; it is simply a means by which a student can be appraised of his level of achievement in academic pursuits. It gives him a chance to reassess his direction

[3]Warren Bryan Martin, "The Ethical Crisis in Education," *Change*, 1974, *6*(5), 30-31.
[4]Edward M. White, "Sometimes an A Is Really an F," *Chronicle of Higher Education*, February 3, 1975.

and to plan for his future, and it may help him determine new strengths or interests. Giving students undeserved recognition may also subvert their incentive to excel, to increasingly gain knowledge and intellectual understanding. It can easily encourage a student to be academically lazy and may dull his sense of curiosity and inquiry. Alan Paskow observed this phenomenon when his students, assured of a passing grade, displayed virtually no interest in going beyond the minimum effort required.[5]

The net effect of arguments against grading is evasion of the responsibility to evaluate students' progress. But Edward White states that "since the evaluative function rests . . . in the professors' pen, it is idle and hypocritical to pretend it does not."[6] And W. T. Lippincot identifies at least three reasons for maintaining traditional standards in student evaluation. First, no viable substitutes have been devised. Second, students can gain a sense of fulfillment through recognition of their competence and of their contributions. Third, educational institutions can provide, through the evaluative process, an indication of the presence of rare talents within a student and a medium for the development of those talents.[7]

Society as well as the student benefits from meaningful academic standards. Not only are colleges and universities responsible for helping students to learn and to achieve their potential, but they are also responsible to the public for certifying at least minimum levels of academic attainment. Such certification is symbolized in the conferral of the degree.[8] Similarly, the conferral of honors should certify distinguished scholarly performance. Each college and university must decide whether it will end the pretense of awarding honors and move into a full-fledged pass-fail or pass-no credit grading system or whether it will return to a realistic evaluation of academic achievement. If the pass-fail system is adopted, faculty members will be relieved both from the pressure of having to carefully criticize a student's work and from the

[5]Alan Paskow, "Are College Students Educable?" *Journal of Higher Education*, 1974, *45*(3), 184-196.

[6]White, "Sometimes an A Is Really an F."

[7]W. T. Lippincot, "On Abandoning Grading and Reconsidering Standards," *Journal of Chemical Education*, 1973, *50*(7), 449.

[8]John Harris, "Baccalaureate Requirements: Attainments or Exposures?" *Educational Record*, 1972, *53*(1), 59-65.

responsibility of acknowledging any level of scholarly achievement beyond the minimum required for satisfactory completion of the program. Students will be relieved from the pressures of having to work hard, to give their best effort. Although outstanding scholarship will not be recognized, no one will be hurt by low quality-point averages because there will be none.

If, however, institutions choose the second path and push for a responsible certification process, faculty members will be challenged to develop course objectives and evaluative criteria and will strive to give an honest appraisal of performance and academic attainment. Students, too, will be motivated to excel in their academic pursuits, and their exceptional scholarship and superior performance will be recognized. Outstanding scholarly achievement that sets a student apart from classmates should be the only standard for awarding honors at commencement. Only when this criterion is reinstated will legitimacy be restored to cum laude, magna cum laude, and summa cum laude.

PART FOUR

Investing
in Futures

XXXXXXXXXXXXXXXXXX

Repentance *is not a mournful word. Traced to its roots, it means
"to think again," or "to think in a new way." During the thirties,
after the stock market crashed, many people repented. They
learned to be less profligate, to proceed with caution, to cultivate
a longer view of the future. When the explosive growth of higher
education suddenly fizzled out in the sixties, educators were
shocked into a similar repentance. They too have cultivated a
longer, more cautious view of the future. What some might label
*experiential learning *could just as well be characterized by an old
saw: you get burned, you learn.*

*Howard R. Bowen, Avery professor of economics and edu-
cation at Claremont Graduate School, takes a wide-angle view of
the year 2000 and considers potential enrollments and probable
instructional methods and financial policy. Acknowledging that
many social, political, and economic variables are beyond the con-*

trol of higher education, Bowen nevertheless sees the destiny of higher education as being largely determined by the incentive or lack of incentive the current leadership shows. A continued effort must be made, he says, to develop the "kinds of institutions and programs that are relevant to the new learners and toward giving the American people a vision of what 'the learning society' might be like." But although he sees new learners and new ways of serving them in the year 2000, Bowen believes that the "traditional financial system of higher education—including low tuitions, student aid in the form of grants, and moderate use of loans—has served us well and should be continued."

Joseph Duffey, general secretary of the American Association of University Professors, is concerned less with structures and numbers than with the character of higher education. Colleges and universities are not threatened from the outside as much as they are from within, Duffey says, and the threat presents itself in the form of timidity, acquiescence, and a "surrender of civic courage and critical judgment." Years from now, he concludes, "The issue will not be whether we have freedom to speak. It will be whether we have anything to say."

Three authors in this part examine state and federal funding policies. L. Richard Meeth, professor of higher education at SUNY Buffalo, discusses the ways in which state funding formulas, developed from traditional educational programs, discriminate against nontraditional programs. He offers a number of suggestions that could, if adopted, give innovative programs the time and support they need in order to demonstrate their effectiveness.

The second author, Carol Van Alstyne, chief economist of the Policy Analysis Service of the American Council on Education, considers the place of higher education among national priorities. She analyzes why higher education is in a slump politically, financially, and publicly, and what steps might be taken to bring it out of the slump. The outlook, she feels, is not as gloomy as educators forecast, but a self-fulfilling prophecy may result unless a more positive attitude is adopted.

Clifton R. Wharton, Jr., president of Michigan State University, believes that instead of holding the line on financial support for postsecondary education, the government should move affirmatively toward a learning society by establishing a citizen's bill of educational entitlement. He estimates the cost of such a program and concludes that the long-range benefits to society would amount to a significant net gain.

All contributors to Part Four probably consider planning the most important function higher education can engage in if it is to shape its own future rather than be shaped by external forces. Willard F. Enteman, provost at Union College, sees planning as not only important but essential, and believes few institutions are putting enough effort, or the right kind of effort, into it. Like Van Alstyne, he sees a pervasive negativism among the leaders of higher education. The result, he says, is habitual, reactive planning rather than creative planning. For Enteman, as for the other contributors to Part Four, the future is not something you back into, it's something you go forth to meet.

William Ferris

16

Teaching and Learning in 2000 A.D.

Howard R. Bowen

W e may be able to judge the potential for change in higher education in the next quarter century by reflecting on the changes that took place in the past twenty-five years. Since 1950, there have been at least four notable developments. The most profound of these has been sheer growth. An elitist and selective higher educational system has been transformed into an open-ended mass system; at the same time, the research functions of higher education have expanded dramatically. To make this growth possible, teachers colleges were converted into state colleges and universities, hundreds of community colleges were formed, new four-year institutions and new branch campuses were established, physical plants were expanded, new programs of financial aid to students were invented and implemented, and the federal government played an ever increasing role in helping to finance higher education—especially in relation to student aid, physical plant, and research.

The second development was a proliferation of new courses and degree programs stemming from the growth of factual knowledge and new professional and semi-professional specialities.

The third development, which has come within the past five years, is that the financial position of higher education has been weakened. This change from financial solvency to serious monetary difficulties reflects the public's doubt and uncertainty about the efficacy of higher education as it now exists and about the direction of its future development.

The fourth development was a profound change in campus life. In 1950, campuses were primarily residential, populated largely by young full-time students, and strongly influenced by the concept of in loco parentis. By 1975, the campuses were serving vast numbers of commuters, including part-time and older students, and the concept of parental supervision had been swept away. In the process, without anyone intending it, the traditional idea about the campus as a closely knit community that influenced student character and outlook was largely abandoned. I estimate that not more than 30 percent of the total higher education enrollment today consists of residential students in closely knit academic communities.

These four changes, profound though they were, did not affect the central functions of teaching and learning very much. During the decade from 1965 to 1975, however, inquiry, research, and invention devoted to teaching-learning in higher education increased greatly. Experimentation with novel concepts and new techniques also increased. Even though genuine and serious innovation is still not the norm at the present time, it appears that it is catching on and that it might be the source of profound changes in the next quarter century.

With this background, I shall explore the possibilities for the next 25 years. What actually happens will depend on the policies we pursue. A specific model of higher education is not foreordained; rather, possibilities range from stagnation to sustained progress in quality, efficiency, and growth. The kinds of social decisions we make will be crucial in determining what possibilities

we will offer potential students, young and old, in higher education. Future changes are likely to occur in the same four areas
mentioned above: enrollments, instructional methods, finances,
and campus environment.

Enrollment predictions can never be precise because they
are based on assumptions about human behavior—behavior that
depends on a multitude of transient influences such as war and
peace, levels of employment, the distribution of income, family
relationships, fashions within peer groups, changing birth rates,
and values relating to income and work. Enrollment predictions
are also based on assumptions about the kind of higher education
that will be offered and the terms on which it is available; again,
we cannot be sure such assumptions are valid. Enrollment predictions based on estimated manpower requirements are equally suspect, partly because the purpose of education is (or should be) to
develop human beings rather than to fill slots in a job market, and
partly because the economy is enormously adaptive to the kinds
of manpower it has.[1] Thus, it is more useful to speak of future
enrollment possibilities than future enrollment predictions. Predictions have the effect of imposing arbitrary ceilings on our aspirations, whereas possibilities are more open-ended and suggest that
we should choose policies that are likely to result in socially desirable enrollment levels.

In comparison with present higher education enrollments
(both part time and full time) of about ten million students, the
potential student body in the year 2000 will consist of the entire
adult population—estimated to be about 190 million persons. Taking into account the benefits and the costs for the nation, how
many of these 190 million adults should receive a higher education? Obviously not all of them can participate in higher education
programs all of the time. Many will be holding down jobs necessary to the functioning of society, many will be pursuing interests
other than education, many will be able to achieve an appropriate
educational level without institutional assistance, and some will
not be able mentally to benefit from higher education. But the
question remains: How many of the estimated 190 million adults
might be participating in formal postsecondary instruction in the

[1] Howard R. Bowen, "Higher Education: A Growth Industry?" *Educational Record*, Summer 1974, 155-158.

year 2000? Only by dealing with this question directly can we begin to comprehend the dimensions of the educational task before us.

In several states in 1972, over 50 percent of the population in the eighteen-to-twenty-four age bracket attended college either full time or part time.[2] Further, 56 percent of the eighteen- to twenty-four-year-olds whose families earned above $15,000 a year were attending college full time.[3] We might project from these figures a full-time-equivalent enrollment of about half of the national population in the eighteen-to-twenty-four age group by the end of the century. Added to the enrollment of older adults, this would mean a total full-time enrollment of perhaps thirteen to fourteen million, or double the present figure. The increases would be due not only to the admission of more people but to the prolongation of education as fewer people became dropouts, as more transferred from community colleges to four-year institutions, and as more pursued advanced study. The total number of enrollees at any time would also increase as more parents, themselves the products of higher education, encouraged their offspring to enter colleges and universities.

In addition, suppose we were to adopt policies that strongly encouraged education of adults beyond the age of twenty-four, of whom there will be about 160 million in the year 2000. Suppose 10 percent of these people took one college course each year. That would produce the equivalent of 2,000,000 full-time students. Suppose also that 3 percent of the 160 million adults over age twenty-four attended college full time for one semester, perhaps under a sabbatical plan; the result would be 2,400,000 full-time equivalent students each year. Add to these figures the possible enrollments in various nondegree credit programs for adults: the potential enrollment in higher education might well reach 18 to 20 million, more than double the present enrollment.

Another way to phrase the question of potential enrollment in higher education is: What proportion of the total adult population is educable at the postsecondary level? Evidence from test

[2] Carnegie Commission on Higher Education, *Priorities for Action: Final Report* (New York: McGraw-Hill, 1973), pp. 101-102.
[3] National Commission on the Financing of Postsecondary Education, *Financing Post-Secondary Education in the United States* (Washington, D.C.: U.S. Government Printing Office, 1973).

scores suggests that this proportion has risen steadily over the years. I have heard one informed guess that as much as 75 to 85 percent of the population might be educable if further improvements are made in childhood education and family and social background, and in adjusting to the higher education system. The potential is clearly far beyond that envisioned in higher education policy today.

I describe enrollments of these magnitudes as possibilities, not projections or predictions. They will occur only if suitable policies are adopted. These policies relate to the kinds of institutions and programs available and to the terms on which education is offered. If the educational system is to serve the needs of large numbers of people, it must provide varied programs and diverse styles of teaching and learning. Admissions requirements must be reasonable and inviting. The education must be interesting, challenging, and relevant to its students. It must be available at convenient times and places. Learning through informal and unorthodox methods must be included. Provisions for released time from work, including sabbatical leaves, must be made. The education must be feasible financially, especially in relation to tuitions and financial aid. Standards must be maintained so that the education is significant and respectable, but the standards must also recognize different kinds of abilities and competencies and avoid narrowness and rigidity.[4]

The policies are not easily translated into operational terms; financial support and practical application will be difficult. As it is currently structured, the higher education community is not well prepared technically, psychologically, or politically for the tasks that lie ahead.

In relation to instructional developments, a substantial foundation has been laid to help accelerate change—partly to improve and diversify instruction and partly to cut costs. The character of teaching-learning in the year 2000 will depend to a large extent on which of the currently successful innovations can best be integrated into the traditional education process.

Programmed independent study is the current vogue. There

[4]K. Patricia Cross, "The Elusive Goal of Educational Quality," Address to American Council on Education, San Diego, California, October 10, 1974.

are many variations on this theme, and there is no limit on the imagination and inventiveness of contemporary educators in devising new systems. The intent of educators is to devise a single program that will guide many students through a course of study by means of a series of operations (reading, listening, problem-solving, writing), while requiring only minimal individual attention from professors. It is hoped that programmed independent study will increase the independence and initiative of students, cut instructional costs, and diversify the modes|of teaching-learning.|

Innovation in instruction faces serious obstacles, however. Evaluating the results of new systems is extraordinarily difficult; the superiority of innovative programs, either in educational effectiveness or cost, is hard to establish. Effectiveness often declines when the newness wears off, or methods that are effective at one time and place may prove to be ineffective at other times and places. New programs are not adopted widely because few faculty are willing to experiment with educational techniques. Under prevailing incentive systems, even professors who are receptive to innovation may eventually lose enthusiasm and retreat to conventional modes of instruction.

Perhaps the greatest obstacle to changes in teaching-learning is financing. The initial investment that new methods require is hard to extract from tight institutional budgets. At the very minimum, change requires a large time investment by some person or group in order to conceive and plan innovations, gain administrative approval, prepare teaching materials or programs, and put the new methods into operation. Change may also call for expensive equipment and building space. Thus, financing is needed for both faculty time and physical facilities. Further complicating the problem is that the initial financial commitments must be made for projects of unknown value. They are therefore risky. Past experience teaches us that most such innovations come to very little. It is the rare one that really pays off. Even for successful programs, life expectancy is often short and the number of students involved is often small; thus, the cost per student turns out to be higher than costs for conventional instruction.

If innovations could be adopted simultaneously in many institutions, just as textbooks are widely used, expenses could be shared and cost per student could be reduced. But such interinstitutional cooperation is difficult to achieve. It helps when foundations supply initial capital, but even then the financial problem is not necessarily solved. Foundation funds have a way of expiring before infant projects grow up. Projects may die for lack of sustenance or continue in a state of anemia if they survive at all.

Fortunately, not all innovations are costly. Some forms of programmed independent study require little more than a syllabus, a library, and some general faculty supervision. Credit by examination and competency-based learning are not necessarily expensive. Breakthroughs in programmed independent study can probably be attributed to the fact that expensive hardware or elaborate and costly software are not always necessary.

Despite the difficulties and the risks, innovation, particularly in programmed independent study, is gaining more and more momentum. I expect this momentum to continue, and I believe it will change the face of higher education significantly by the year 2000. In the process of development, costs and risks will diminish, and it may even become feasible to use some expensive hardware. I do not expect the newer methods to replace traditional higher education programs; rather, I expect them to be mixed with conventional methods to increase learning options.[5]

An important extension of the teaching-learning process is the extracurricular environment. Changes in this environment, the fourth major development in higher education, have had and will have a significant impact. A generation ago, most educators thought that a well designed campus life helped to direct students toward desirable goals. They spent much effort and a good deal of money shaping campus environments that they felt would exert a civilizing influence, mold desirable character, and cultivate the social graces. Today, such goals are played down even in the old-line residential colleges. The overthrow of in loco parentis, the growth of many institutions in sheer size, the rise of two-year and four-year urban commuter institutions, the cost squeeze that has eliminated some of the niceties of college life, and the spread of egalitarian sentiments—all have helped to reduce the influence of the campus community. Even the Carnegie Commission has warned against "totalism" and has advised that "the college should not assume the full developmental responsibility for students."[6]

[5] Howard R. Bowen and Gordon K. Douglass, *Efficiency in Liberal Education* (New York: McGraw-Hill, 1971).
[6] Carnegie Commission on Higher Education, *The Purposes and Per-*

This apparent decline in the degree to which campus community life influences personality, character, values, and social graces means that higher education is thought of increasingly as academic education that can be measured solely in credits earned and not in years of residence on a campus or participation in a college community. Credits become the sole building blocks of an education. Innovations such as programmed independent study or mechanical means of delivery fit into this concept of a college education very easily. These innovations fulfill specific course or competency requirements and thus generate credits. They are usually evaluated by comparing test results from the new and the old methods. I consider it unfortunate, however, that little or no effort is made to discover and evaluate what is happening to the whole person as he moves through the process, or what kind of human being is likely to emerge from the total experience. I am not suggesting that the paternalistic and elitist residential campuses of earlier generations be recreated. My point is that mass enrollments and innovative new methods do not exempt the higher education system from being concerned about the whole person or from finding ways to express that concern. A concept of education based merely on the accumulation of credits is doomed not merely to failure but to disaster.

Perhaps the campus environment can continue to involve the whole person by using the resources of urban society to greater advantage than it has in the past. Every city offers libraries, museums, concerts, plays, lectures, churches, clubs, desirable role models for youth, and desirable peer influences. Although such external resources should be tapped as much as possible, I think colleges and universities should continue to be campus-centered communities that administer to both the intellectual and personal development of their students. Institutional higher education offers many advantages. It provides libraries, laboratories, studios, stimulating peers, skilled teachers who may serve as role models as well as instructors, suitable physical space and equipment, systematic plans of teaching-learning, guidance, and an extracurricular campus life. This is not to say that no teaching-learning should occur elsewhere; it is to say that the campus is on the whole a

formance of Higher Education in the United States (New York: McGraw-Hill, 1974), p. 17.

superior learning environment and when convenient will tend to be used. For example, I doubt that external study will become a dominant form of instruction. I expect it to grow in scope and influence but mostly in combination with campus-based instruction. During the last twenty-five years, the nation has created a system of campuses that are within commuting distance of some 90 percent of the entire population. These campuses are a resource of inestimable value and they should be used.

I have suggested that enrollment could expand significantly, new educational techniques may be ready for exploitation, and that higher education may continue to be concerned with the personal as well as intellectual development of its students during the next quarter century. This scenario for the future will, of course, raise total expenses enormously—even in terms of constant dollars. Moreover, it will probably not result in reductions in per student costs. If enrollment doubles, total expenses will probably more than double. The most optimistic outcome I can envision is that the rapid rise in cost per student experienced during the last quarter century will slow down and eventually level off. I expect this leveling off to occur for two reasons.

First, the present financial squeeze is forcing reductions in expenditures. The money spent on higher education is partly determined by how much money can be raised. Thus, if available funds do not keep pace with increases in the number of enrollees, cost per student must decrease.[7] Some reductions can be achieved through higher ratios of students to teachers, by streamlining programs, and through innovations such as programmed independent study and mechanical delivery systems. However, these methods may be less cost efficient than they are sometimes claimed to be. First, higher education has already experienced several years of severe budgetary pressure, and much of the fat has been pared away. Second, newer methods of instruction are usually not very cost-saving in the early stages of their development.[8] And finally, education of satisfactory quality cannot be provided without

[7]G. R. Wynn, *At the Crossroads: A Report on the Financial Condition of Forty-eight Liberal Arts Colleges* (Ann Arbor: University of Michigan, 1974).
[8]Bowen and Douglass, *Efficiency in Liberal Education*; and Howard R. Bowen, "Financing the External Degree," *Journal of Higher Education*, Summer 1973.

personal attention to the individual, and personal attention also requires financing.

My second reason for a leveling off in cost increases is that I expect the whole economy to slow down. Natural resources and the capacity of the environment to absorb pollution will be limited. Growth in the production rate of physical goods will be valued less than it has been in the past. The nation will turn increasingly to the production of personal services where technological progress is slow. Because of these factors, wages and salaries generally will rise less rapidly (in constant dollars) than in the past, and so the costs of higher education—which consist largely of wages and salaries—will also rise less rapidly.

Although I expect the persistent rise in cost per student to level off, I believe the concept of education of acceptable quality precludes significant cost reductions. Can society afford the continued expenses of higher education? *Afford* is a slippery word. In both our personal and our social budgets, we can afford our priorities. If the priorities of potential students and society, as expressed mainly in the political process at the state and federal levels, include higher education of high quality, we shall be able to afford it. But if our priorities center on national economic growth, then I would expect that we might view further expansion of higher education as too expensive.

The most significant contributions that higher education could make in the future are, I believe, to help individuals reach their fullest potential, to enrich the culture, and to make equality of opportunity and attainment a reality—not to aid the growth of the gross national product. The question is whether a society that has been conditioned to value higher education for its economic benefits will value higher education for its contributions to the development of individual human beings and to the creation of a humane society. The true crisis faced by higher education today is whether it can be liberated from its deep involvement with economic goals. In saying this, I do not suggest that education and economic development are or will be unrelated. And I do not suggest that educated people will have no work to do. I am saying that the differential advantage in the labor market enjoyed by college-educated people—some of it due to education per se and some to the sorting and screening function of higher education—will narrow and eventually disappear. I look upon this possibility as a desirable outcome. It will mean that technology will be marshalled to do away with the backbreaking, stultifying, and demeaning jobs in our society because there will be no one willing to occupy them; and it will mean that the invidious distinctions between blue-collar and white-collar work will cease to exist. It could mean that careers will be chosen according to personal interests and not according to potential income or status. It could also mean that higher education would focus increasingly on developing intelligent and humane people and on advancing civilization rather than on developing the economy. In other words, universal education is one route toward the classless society. But are the American people, individually and collectively, ready for this concept of education?

If higher education is to develop according to the possibilities I have outlined, then the nation must provide many varied institutions suited to the next generation of learners, and it must make higher education available on terms that encourage rather than restrict participation. Finally, this means moderate tuitions and generous student aid that does not rely so heavily on loans so as to create an unworkable system of public welfare tied to higher education. Higher education policy in the United States has been moving in these directions since its beginning. Presently, however, we are tempted to deviate from this traditional policy. We talk of curtailing further growth of higher education. We are worried lest there be too many educated people—by which we really mean that we want to maintain a large enough supply of docile and ignorant workers to fill the menial jobs. We speak of high tuitions, full-cost pricing, and extensive use of loans as the ways to finance higher education.

I do not know whether these views will prevail, but I think there is a chance that the less privileged members of our society will press for the education to which they are entitled. If our society devotes itself seriously to solving the great social and economic problems we face, the need for educated workers will be very great. If our society is engaged increasingly in the production of services rather than goods and if it allows itself increasing leisure, people will turn to higher education as a preferred activity and the concept of "the learning society" might be realized. Whether these things happen will depend in part on the leadership of higher education. This leadership must be exerted toward inventing the kinds of institutions and programs that are relevant to the new learners and toward giving the American people a vision of what "the learning society" might be like.

In the next quarter century, there might very well be a vast number of learners who are no longer youthful. Helping them to gain access to higher education will require forms of financial aid that have not yet been invented. The basic requirements are low tuitions and student aid to meet expenses or to replace income lost during periods of full-time education. Questions like these must be answered: Who is to replace the salary of a middle-aged person who wishes to spend a semester or year in concentrated education in order to complete work toward a degree? Who is to pay the tuitions and other educational expenses of a housewife who wishes to resume her education but who has three children at or nearing college age? Who is to pay the tuition of an elderly person of modest income who wishes to use his retirement leisure for learning? Should college students of any age over eighteen be regarded as independent adults, as they are indeed regarded in law, or should they be regarded as dependent on their families? If they are dependent, does the education of youths take priority over that of parents? So far, our society has given these questions little attention.

There is talk of asking industry to provide sabbaticals for its employees. If that is done, consumers will end up paying for it by higher prices on the things they buy. There is talk of providing a lifetime entitlement to a certain amount of education or other self-development, the entitlement to be financed by government. But costs undoubtedly will prove to be high, and the nation may be slow in moving into these areas. I would expect considerable progress in relation to the more modest measures, however. I would also expect some shortening of the work week and the work year, and I would expect the higher education system to provide education at convenient times and places, in forms that could attract millions of adults beyond the usual college age, and at low tuitions.

In conclusion, I believe the traditional system of higher education, if it remains flexible, can meet the future educational needs of both young adults and older adults. The traditional financial system of higher education—including low tuitions, student aid in the form of grants, and moderate use of loans—has served us well and should be continued. It should be able to deal successfully with the requirements of learner-centered reform.

17

Future of the Professoriate

Joseph D. Duffey

W e all have heard or read explanations for what some call *faculty militance*. As one observer put it recently, "College teachers these days are getting to be a feisty bunch." I have read psychological analyses and organizational theories that attempt to explain why this is happening. Some of my friends in administrative posts have expressed their consternation at what they see as a growing sense of adversarial relationships between faculty members and administrators, which more and more seem to be leading to collective bargaining on the campus.

I do not believe this restlessness, this new *militance*—if that is an apt term for it—stems from any deep psychological unhappiness, or from an innate conservatism among faculty. Academic reformers who begin with such an analysis are off the mark. Too many publications about the malaise of higher education in recent years have employed a simplistic analysis that paints the faculty as the source of the trouble. A good example is Lewis Mayhew's book, *Arrogance on Campus*. While generally a well balanced discussion of some of the problems of academic performance, this book is quick to single out faculty as the bête noire of most institutional ills. Consider the following analysis:

"Feelings of powerlessness on the part of professors are aggravated by an underlying feeling of insecurity which seems endemic in academic man. Sociologists describe marginal men as people who have left one group or culture and who are striving to enter another but do not make it. Marginal people are characterized by feelings of frustration, and quite often rage. In a sense many academic men are marginal. Some, with lower class backgrounds, use intelligence and education to move into the higher classes of society. As college professors, they have many of the attributes of the higher classes but still do not make important social, economic, or political decisions. . . . The result is these feelings of insecurity and anxiety which professors seek to relieve through striking out at the system or organizing to defeat it."[1]

In another passage, Mayhew writes: "Among traditional vices faculty conservatism is the most endemic and hurtful. College professors do not like educational change and will not undertake it unless forced by an external power (for example, students), bribed by financial inducements, or persuaded by powerful leaders. The great innovations in higher education were all generated outside the faculty and imposed over faculty opposition."[2]

Mayhew's analysis reflects the views of a good number of those who offer prescriptions about the future of the academy. Although such views of higher education today may be in part accurate, they are flawed by social and intellectual biases of no small magnitude. Let me first take up the social bias. Many who comment on the responsibilities of the professoriate fail to consider the economic insecurity of a good number of college teachers, especially the younger ones. The decade of the 1960s resulted

---

[1] Lewis B. Mayhew, *Arrogance on Campus* (San Francisco: Jossey-Bass, 1970), p. 69.

[2] Mayhew, p. 80.

in a significant improvement in faculty compensation. When we look at the surveys of faculty salaries, the first impression is that things are not so bad. But consider that our perspective is often based on salary scales of some of the major state universities and college systems and on the assumption that most faculty have extra opportunities to earn income through consulting or summer teaching.

The data on faculty income and "extra" income are not too precise, but two conclusions are consistent with what we do know. First, more than half of those who teach in our colleges and universities have no opportunity to earn extra income by summer teaching or through the high-paid consultations that we hear so much about. Second, nearly a third of the college and university teachers in America today are earning an income below the national family average income—that is, below the level of approximately $13,500.

There is a widespread tendency to characterize the American social scene by referring to truck drivers who earn $20,000 a year, sanitation workers who earn $15,000, or professors who earn $30,000. All these examples exist. But all are exceptions that distort our perception of social reality. Many truck drivers earn less than half of that $20,000; most sanitation workers in this country earn not much more than welfare benefits; and most college teachers are not flying around the country picking up high consultation fees—some traditions in the Ivy League and the Big Ten notwithstanding. Those who puzzle over a certain new sense of faculty frustration ought to bear in mind the serious economic plight of many young teachers in America and their perception that things are not likely to get much better.

As for the second charge commonly leveled against faculty—that they have been indifferent if not resistant to educational reform—I would again caution against simplistic analysis. Reform in American higher education is only one aspect of urgently needed social and economic reform. Education is not a lever for broad social reform; rather, it is one of many strands of our cultural life which must somehow be untangled and rewoven into a more humane and liberating pattern. Many of those who talk of higher education reform are naive about the ways in which institutional behavior breeds faculty unrest. Widespread naivete on the part of instructors and administrators prevents them from meeting and resolving the conflict in the university. They fail to acknowledge the truly corporate nature of the institutions to which they are related. Faculty sometimes talk and act as if they are free-floating entrepreneurs, when they are, in fact, facing a public that demands a much more explicit rationale for continuing to pay the rising costs of higher education. The public is not only demanding such a rationale but is willing to listen to it as well. And it is more receptive to talk of values, of the need for independence in our centers of learning, and of the importance of general education than most educators would assume. The public today asks for a rationale for higher education and is too often shown only budget charts. But not only faculty members are naive. Administrators and trustees are tempted to cling to the myths of an earlier era. Some envision a community of learning and research free from the stringent public scrutiny and skepticism that is directed toward all institutions today.

Further underscoring the corporate nature of higher education is the fact that both public and independent universities have emerged as major employers. In construction, housing, food services, security, and recreation, as well as educational offerings, they are complex corporate structures. They require methods of governance and management different from those that the bureaucratic college oligarchies required in the past. Too often, trustees and administrators assume that the educational mission of their colleges and universities exempts them from the social responsibilities expected of industry. Although a president or a trustee would be shocked if a local industrial firm laid off a thirty-year employee who had little prospect of finding another position, they might accept that kind of behavior from a college without qualms.

There has been much talk recently of the problems of accountability in education, especially higher education. The single word *accountability* intimidates the faculty, demoralizes the deans, and sends presidents and chancellors into early retirement. It is the word used by those who would disguise traditional do-nothingism as a vigilant protection of the public interest. It is the weapon sometimes used by one part of the academy to attack another part. Still, it is probably the best word available to describe the plight and dilemma of the total community and of those who have a stake in and concern for the future of higher education.

The plight of the university community is a concern shared by all participants. We must acknowledge, however, that both the purpose and the efficient operation of institutions are common responsibilities. There is now, and will be in the future, a sense of adversarial roles involved in fulfilling those responsibilities. There are those who deplore the development of adversarial relationships not only in the academy but also in the society at large. They plead for a return to the days of paternal benevolence, of informal arrangements of mutual trust unacknowledged by explicit, upfront procedures for all to see. But they plead for a return to days that never were.

It is both inevitable and healthy that we play adversarial roles. We need to structure the life of the academy by basic institutional reforms in the way we relate to each other as well as by instructional innovations. Different interests and perspectives can merge into a common concern for learning. Faculty, administration, and students, in healthy adversarial arrangements, should challenge each other with claims of responsibility. Such open give-and-take within the academy, conducted with civility and compromise, will do the most for the future of higher education in the long run.

In the present stage, when we are only now learning to live with these new and, in most cases, unacknowledged realities, there is much posturing and oversimplification on all sides. Sometimes faculty representatives talk about the "power structure" within their institution as if they were only employees. Yet, at the same time, they claim—as I believe they should—basic prerogatives for the exercise of professional judgment and responsibility. And some administrators wring their hands at the need to make explicit institutional demands of the faculty. I agree with Lance Liebman of the Harvard Law School, who has called for more "explicitness" in defining our internal relationships, "our understandings of what we are about and how we go about our business." As Liebman puts it: "The point is rather that a period of explicitness is now arriving at colleges, long a bastion of honest statement about Senegal and Baudelaire and the atom, but a silent, cabalistic ritual in its internal affairs."[3]

Just as the faculty are insisting on greater accountability on

----

[3] Unpublished paper prepared for Carnegie Corporation Project on Collective Bargaining in Higher Education, 1974.

the part of institutions, so will faculty accountability be demanded. Most professional groups in our society need such structural demands to ensure responsible performance. And most professional communities resist such arrangements, not as much out of human perversity as out of self-interest. But the challenge that faces our society and those who care about the professions—whether medicine, law, or teaching—is to find structural arrangements that protect the integrity of such professions without isolating them from the public demand for accountability. Faculty accountability will not be achieved, however, by increasing faculty insecurity. Too many recent treatises on educational reform in America have been built on the central assumption that the single most important innovation for the future well-being of higher education would be to abolish tenure commitments to the faculty in order to ensure "flexibility in planning" for administrators.

There is to my mind no single arena in America where the human capacity for self-governance and civil dialogue will be more clearly revealed in the next decade than on the campuses of our colleges and universities. I say that even though I am convinced that campuses are basically at the mercy of whatever happens in the society at large. The major issues in our society are no longer those dealing with our right to govern ourselves or the necessity for civil discourse, negotiation, and compromise in the interest of sharing power and authority. Rather, they are those dealing with our capacity and our will to govern ourselves. The question, then, is whether or not we have the capacity for the restraint, the energy, the determination, the care, and the sensitivity necessary to shape our own destinies.

The AAUP has been deeply involved for six decades in trying to state the nature and responsibilities of what we call academic freedom. These efforts continue today in a new and changing environment. I hope that in the process of reforming our curricula to adapt to new societal needs, we will not lose sight of another significant function of higher education. I refer to the fact that the higher education community has been, and must remain, a center for challenging and questioning the conventional wisdom of the society. The 1960s represented a decade of debate about the relation between scholarship and political activism, and the academy today is still deeply divided over questions concerning objectivity and values.

There are times when attacks or intimidation by those out-

side the academic community do not threaten academic freedom
as much as does timidity or acquiescence within our own ranks. I
believe this is such a time. One of the social functions of higher
education is to provide the skills demanded by a changing economic process. But the most important function of higher education is to encourage values that will enable the citizenry to shape
the processes of economic development rather than be shaped by
them.

The vision I have of the dilemmas of academic freedom in
the future was expressed over 140 years ago by Alexis de Tocqueville in *Democracy in America*. In an incredibly prophetic passage,
"What Sort of Despotism Democratic Nations Have to Fear," de
Tocqueville anticipated the central problem of academic freedom
in our time: not a confrontation with external repression but the
consequences of the surrender of civic courage and critical judgment. He wrote:

*I seek to trace the novel features under which despotism
may appear in the world. The first thing that strikes the observation is an innumerable multitude of men, all equal and alike, inces-
santly endeavoring to procure . . . pleasures with which they glut
their lives. Each of them, living apart, is a stranger to the fate of all
the rest—his children and his private friends constitute to him the
whole of mankind; as for the rest of his fellow-citizens, he is close
to them, but he sees them not—he touches them, but he feels them
not; he exists but in himself and for himself alone; and if his kin-
dred still remain to him, he may be said, at any rate, to have lost
his country.*

*Above this race of men stands an immense . . . power which
takes upon itself alone to secure their gratifications and to watch
over their fate. That power is absolute . . . regular, provident, and
mild. It would be like the authority of a parent, if, like that authority, its object was to prepare men for manhood; but it seeks,
on the contrary, to keep them in perpetual childhood; it is well
content that the people should rejoice, provided they think of
nothing but rejoicing. For their happiness such a government will-
ingly labors, but it chooses to be the sole agent and the only arbi-
ter of that happiness; it provides for their security, foresees and
supplies their necessities, facilitates their pleasures, manages their
principal concerns. . . . What remains but to spare them all the care
of thinking and all the trouble of living? . . .*

*The will of man is not shattered but softened, bent, and
guided; men are seldom forced by it to act, but they are con-*

stantly restrained from acting. Such a power does not destroy, but it prevents existence; it does not tyrannize, but it compresses, enervates, extinguishes, and stupefies a people, till each nation is reduced to be nothing better than a flock of timid and industrious animals, of which the government is the shepherd.

I have always thought that servitude of the regular, quiet, and gentle kind which I have just described might be combined more easily than is commonly believed with some of the outward forms of freedom and that it might even establish itself under the wing of the soveriegnty of the people.

The kind of future de Tocqueville envisioned will be, I believe, the challenge for those who seek to preserve academic freedom. The issue will not be whether we have the freedom to speak. It will be whether we have anything to say.

18

Restrictive Practices in Formula Funding

L. Richard Meeth

Innovative programs in American postsecondary education are not always received with open arms by traditional faculty, administrators, state boards, or legislators. Sometimes these programs have been tolerated, sometimes encouraged, sometimes prematurely forced to justify their existence, and sometimes thrust onto reluctant institutions by state boards. Even though innovative programs are by definition nontraditional, they compete with traditional education for funding and are accorded or denied it by the same criteria. Since the programs are largely efforts to explore and demonstrate effective teaching and learning not present in traditional postsecondary education, we may question how appropriate it is to judge their financial right to life by traditional standards.

To gather information on the range of state and federal funding problems being experienced by nontraditional education in the United States, lengthy interviews were conducted with administrators of several programs: College IV of Grand Valley State in Michigan, the experimental colleges of the State University of New York at Buffalo, the external degree program of Empire State College in New York, the modularized general education program at Bowling Green State University in Ohio, College III of the University of Massachusetts at Boston; and the external degree program of the Community College of Vermont.

In addition, a questionnaire was mailed to over 300 nontraditional programs identified as "new or unconventional forms of postsecondary education free of traditional time or place limitations."[1] Of these questionnaires, 134 were returned; 48 respondents indicated some serious problem with state or federal funding formulas and 86 reported no particular problems with funding. Even though few programs cited serious difficulty, many more have experienced financial problems and have compromised their integrity in order to exist. Others would have experienced the problems, if they had not felt the obstacles were too great even to begin a program. In fairness, others have had no problems because of very cooperative state boards and legislatures.[2]

Of those programs reporting great difficulty with state or federal funding agencies, 70 percent were public and 30 percent private—about the same percentage as the public-private ratio in the total responses. Almost 85 percent of the programs with funding problems were parts of traditional institutions—again a percentage similar to the percentage of such programs in the total response. Thus, public college and university programs operating within larger traditional schools seem to have the greatest difficulty with funding guidelines.

In addition to being queried about guideline problems, directors of nontraditional programs were asked about other problems with state and federal agencies. In this connection, half the

[1]K. Patricia Cross, John R. Valley, and Associates, *Planning Non-Traditional Programs: An Analysis of the Issues for Postsecondary Education* (San Francisco: Jossey-Bass, 1974), p. 380.
[2]The study was conducted by the author for the Institute for Educational Leadership of The George Washington University, under a grant from the Fund for the Improvement of Postsecondary Education.

respondents reported problems related to program approval, program exclusion, and faculty work requirements.

Before we consider the funding problems of nontraditional programs, it might be useful to review briefly the formulas from which many of the problems arise. Formulas or guidelines are used in two-thirds of the states. In 1973, twenty-five states used formulas, eight had guidelines similar to the formulas but not as comprehensive, and three states used program budgeting.[3] Eight other states, which had previously used budget formulas for allocating funds to institutions of higher education, had abandoned the practice by 1973.

These formulas are complex. As with every technical field, a highly specialized language has developed that is somewhat difficult for outsiders to understand. Three basic computational methods are employed. The first is the rate per base factor, which means that a university's operating costs of the preceding year, divided by such measures as credit hours, and square feet, are multipled by a fixed rate of increase to determine the budget for the current year. Thus, if instructional salaries were a million dollars the year before and the rate is 1.10, the salaries will go up one hundred thousand dollars. The second formula is the percentage of base factor, which is a straight percentage increase over the previous year's costs, again computed by unit measures such as full-time-equivalent students. The third formula, the base factor-position ratio, is the preceding year's costs shaped by separately established student-faculty ratios and salary rates. This computational method takes into account fluctuating enrollment. For example, if the number of full-time students decrease, the state can maintain the ratio and cut faculty or change the ratio and maintain the faculty.[4]

No state uses all three methods, nor do all states use any one method. Computation by the percentage of base factor is most commonly used to estimate funds for organized activities related to instruction. This category, of great concern to nontraditional programs, covers departmental research, faculty and related

[3] Francis McK. Gross, *A Comparative Analysis of the Existing Budget Formulas Used for Justifying Budget Requests or Allocating Funds for the Operating Expenses of State Supported Colleges and Universities*, unpublished dissertation, University of Tennessee, 1973, p. iv.
    [4] Gross, p. v.

staff salaries, and direct instructional expenses incurred by departments. The difference between base-factor computations and zero-base-factor computations is another important concept in formula budgeting. Budgets are built either on the previous year's costs or the costs are recomputed annually without including any percentage or rate increase over the previous year. The first formula is the base-factor method and the second the zero-base-factor method.

The pros and cons of budget formulas have been argued strongly for a number of years and the debate continues—even though several states, deciding that the disadvantages outweighed the advantages, discontinued formulas. Supporters of budget formulas believe that: such formulas provide an objective measure of the funding requirements of college and university programs since they do not rely on the judgments of program officers and administrators; budget formulas can reduce open competition among institutions for state funds and can assure each institution of an annual operating appropriation; budget formulas provide state officials with a reasonably understandable basis for determining the financial needs of higher education; and budget formulas provide a balance between state control over each item in a budget and total institutional autonomy in fiscal matters.

On close examination, however, we find that state and federal funding policies restrain nontraditional programs in a variety of ways. Most of the problems with funding formulas and guidelines grow out of the assumptions on which they are based—the course credit hour or the student credit hour as the fundamental unit of fund determination. Nine to fifteen credit hours equals a full-time-equivalent student. A certain number of full-time-equivalent students or student credit hours determines the number of full-time-equivalent faculty who can be supported. Even though, in most instances, funding is based either on full-time-equivalent students or full-time-equivalent faculty, both of these methods use the credit hour as the basic unit of fund allocation. The problem is that many nontraditional curricula—including competency-based designs, individualized modules, learning contracts, and external degree programs—do not use credit hours. Frequently, programs that include community service or work experiences also have no credit-hour equivalents. In half the states, these nontraditional programs are penalized because the very basis for determining budgets is not an integral part of their design. Even those individualized programs that do use credit hours often cannot generate enough student credit hours to get funding for all the faculty positions necessary to teach in the self-paced program. But no state has devised a unit of measure to replace the credit hour. As a consequence, in states with funding formulas or guidelines, programs that do not use the traditional measure of achievement adopted by the state funding agency often are underfunded; thus, they are denied a chance to demonstrate their full effectiveness.

Another problem is that most funding formulas that use credit hours do so on partial enrollments. Because only fall term figures are used as the basis of support, traditional programs stand to benefit since they typically enroll more students in the first term than in subsequent ones. But this is not the case for some nontraditional institutions. External degree programs, in particular, have found that the smallest enrollments occur in the fall; thus, the money allocated through formulas and direct state aid is less than if a different measure were to be used.

To deal with the credit-hour problem, a number of nontraditional programs are forced to develop an extra bookkeeping system. In addition to recording contact hours (or other faculty workload figures) and achievement units assessed from specified learning outcomes, they must devise a set of credits to report to the funding agency. This activity is not illegal, and may not be unethical in states where it is practiced, but it is confusing and wasteful to justify programs to the state on one set of criteria, to keep the administration and faculty informed on another set of criteria, and to prepare student transcripts on a third set.

Nontraditional programs experience other problems with formulas besides the credit-hour requirement. For example, the practice of using full-time-equivalent students as a basis for determining full-time faculty does not take into account the special nature of some nontraditional programs. In the external degree program at Empire State College, which enrolls large numbers of part-time students, almost as much faculty time and effort are needed to facilitate learning for a part-time student as for a full-time student. Thus, when the number of part-time-equivalent students are used to determine funds for faculty, not enough dollars are generated to handle the real faculty workload.

Some formulas and guidelines forbid money allocated in one category to be used in another. This kind of inflexibility within funding guidelines can, in some instances, prevent administrators of nontraditional programs from using more efficient educational methods. In New York, for example, paraprofessionals cannot be paid from the faculty salary budget. Thus, the director of the experimental colleges at the State University of New York at Buffalo cannot pay undergraduates as peer teachers out of teaching funds because the undergraduates do not "qualify," yet peer teaching in other situations has proved to be a way to reduce costs, increase the student-faculty ratio, and produce as much learning as faculty teaching.

In states with direct grants for private colleges (and twelve states now provide such aid for some or all undergraduate programs), almost all funds awarded are based on full-time campus study. These restrictions eliminate external degree programs, independent study, television and correspondence programs, part-time students, and persons in prisons, retirement homes, nursing homes, and other situations that curtail travel to a campus. Because no state funds are available for part-time or off-campus study in private institutions, these schools are unable to establish many kinds of innovative programs. The tuition that would be needed to cover the cost would discourage enrollment. Thus, while direct state grants benefit full-time, on-campus nontraditional programs, they do little for less expensive, more accessible kinds of innovations and tend to disenfranchise educationally large groups of home- or prison-bound learners.

Even in public colleges, some state formulas and guidelines require on-campus full-time study. Arkansas, California, and Illinois, for example, have this requirement, although it has been contested in Illinois in recent months. Such fiscal control inhibits learning flexibility and the development of less expensive programs that may very well produce equal learning without large capital.

In thirteen states, problems arise because of the way formulas and direct aid provisions differentiate among levels of study within colleges and universities. The first two years of undergraduate study are supported at a set rate based on large lectures and high student-faculty ratios; the rate is increased for the last two undergraduate years and further increased for work at the master's and doctor's levels. Nontraditional general education programs or other nondegree programs do not always have a high student-faculty ratio in the first two years of study. Consequently, many nontraditional programs cannot possibly generate sufficient credit hours to support the faculty needed to teach the curriculum they offer.

External degree programs operating regionally or nationally have an added difficulty. Direct state aid or even state grants is usually not available for students who reside in those states where regional external degree centers are located. Perhaps the best illustration of this problem is the Antioch University Without Walls, which operates many different programs internationally. Maryland residents who attend the Maryland Antioch center cannot receive state tuition grants because the program is based administratively outside the state or because they are not full-time students or are not studying on approved campuses. This same kind of problem prevails in other states and in other institutions. Thus, programs are penalized that cut across state boundaries to provide learning in specialized areas at reduced or no cost to those states.

Other problems arise from basing student aid or direct state aid on college charges, a practice that often reduces the incentive to keep institutional costs down. Neither base-factor budgeting with an annual percentage increase nor zero-based budgeting have any cost effectiveness or efficiency criteria built into them in most states. The irony is that colleges trying to control costs are discouraged from doing so by both state and federal formulas. Berea College in Kentucky, for example, traditionally has charged no tuition and a very low room and board fee for students of limited economic means from the Appalachian region. Each student works ten hours a week in lieu of paying tuition at Berea College. But since state and federal aid to students are based on tuition and room and board charges, those students who would qualify for full aid at another institution get almost no assistance at Berea; the college must continue to raise hundreds of thousands of dollars from private sources to maintain the low tuition and self-help program. State and federal programs, designed to support such efforts, appear to be discouraging them in this case.

Not all of the problems with funding are limited to state formulas and guidelines. At least three serious problems have surfaced as a result of restrictive policies related to federal funding. Currently, the most widely discussed restriction is the policy written into the Federal Register late in 1974 and again in 1975 prohibiting veterans from collecting benefits for independent study and other off-campus external degree programs. Understandably, some recent unethical activity has embarrassed a number of institutions as well as the Veterans Administration. To restrict veterans benefits for those who choose to participate in recognized external degree programs, such as those at Empire State, Minnesota Metropolitan, and Community College of Vermont, or for veterans who choose independent study activities or individualized modular programs off-campus in more traditional institutions, is to throw out the baby with the bath water.

A number of institutions, including the University of Kentucky, also mentioned a problem with federal funding guidelines for work-study. These guidelines placed far too many restrictions on nontraditional learners. Work-study guidelines require students to be enrolled full time, but many nontraditional programs are designed to accommodate part-time learners who need to work. Such students could not easily earn enough money from work-study to remain in some nontraditional programs even if they were eligible for part-time study benefits. Where the costs are passed on to the students in private colleges, part-time students cannot put together a large enough financial aid package to support themselves because of so many restrictions. Since some students cannot afford to attend full time, they are eliminated from many good nontraditional learning opportunities. In a real sense, work-study disqualifies the poor, older adult from many opportunities designed especially to facilitate his or her economic and educational development.

Finally, some institutions have had difficulty because the Department of Labor has not clearly defined the minimum wage for persons who are both students and workers. Individuals who go to college part-time and work part-time at the college may not be eligible for the full minimum wage. Until this problem is clarified, institutions will not know what to pay employees who also study or students who also work.

A number of partial or full remedies to these funding restraints on time- and place-free, innovative educational programs have been proposed by administrators who have experienced the problems as well as by interested external parties. Although the problems of many programs tend to be similar, no single solution is likely. Some of the proposed solutions fit particular situations and would not necessarily be useful in all states. Others have not been put into practice by any institution, and still others depend on cooperation from state officials or legislatures. The following list begins with partial, less appropriate solutions and concludes with recommendations for more far-reaching and potentially effective measures:

Passing the costs on to the students is a course of action that a number colleges—in New York and Michigan, for example—have been forced to choose. College IV of Grand Valley State College prepares and sells curriculum materials to students to help pay extra faculty and resource persons. This method of raising funds is possible because the students cannot function in College IV without the curriculum materials that the institution sells. Colleges without such entrepreneurial leadership have simply raised their tuition for nontraditional programs. Charges as high as $60 per hour have been reported by some public institutions, which recognize that such fees virtually eliminate students from their programs and, in effect, dictate an early demise of the innovation.

"Soft" money has paid start-up costs for a number of programs recently. Private foundations, corporations, and federal programs have awarded many grants to innovative time- and space-free programs in the past five years. The *Yellow Pages of Undergraduate Innovations* documents the large number of programs born through private philanthropy or public grants. The presently depressed economy, however, has reduced corporate and foundation funding and has brought about a significant increase in requests, according to a number of foundation executives. This situation means that nontraditional programs must compete even more fiercely in order to survive. When existence depends on the largesse of the federal government or private philanthropy, unproven programs are not likely to continue for very long.

Several institutions have indicated that they plan to *institute a program of political pressure on state legislators and federal congressmen* in order to bring about some change in state and federal funding bases. But such a plan is more a strategy than a solution to the problems of restrictive funding formulas. Political lobbying is a dangerous enterprise for tax-exempt educational institutions. Nevertheless, public and private colleges and their supporting councils have applied, and will continue to apply, political pressure as a means of securing funding or changing budget procedures to make funding more favorable within a state.

Some educators have recommended that the most appropriate solution to state and federal funding restrictions is to *do away with the formulas and guidelines entirely* and let every college and university program be judged on its own merit. At least eight states that once had formulas have terminated them, although there is no evidence that this action was in any way based on a desire to increase allocations for nontraditional programs. Nevertheless, nontraditional programs may indeed benefit if they have strong advocates in the right courts. On the other hand, they may be eliminated altogether. In many states that have never had funding guidelines, colleges and universities are single lines in an annual or biannual state budget; thus, they are able to develop whatever innovative programs institutional forces will sanction and legislators will fund.

A large number of respondents to the questionnaire indicated that *good will has been an effective substitute for technical solutions* to problems presented by state funding formulas. Some program directors reported that both institutional and statewide administrative interpretation of otherwise inflexible guidelines was enough to overcome most problems they encountered. Sometimes, nontraditional programs that have experienced particular difficulty with state guidelines have not had strong support from the central administrations of their institutions. Some nontraditional programs, for example, have virtually no problem with funding formulas whereas others in the same state have tremendous difficulty.

A vivid illustration of how administrative good will can be lacking was provided by two respondents from a state university. By accident, one questionnaire was sent to the president's office and another to the program director of the university's experimental college. According to the program director, "if our nontraditional program were not included in the general fund, other departments would be more successful because they would not have to compete with us." Such a situation, he said, "gives rise to intrainstitutional suspicion and the administration does not give us much support in these instances." That response turns out to be an understatement since the special assistant to the president returned a blank questionnaire stating that the university offers no nontraditional programs. There is no substitute for trust and good will in the educational enterprise.

Arbitrarily assigning credit hours to everything done in

time- and place-free programs is another solution. Such action is, of course, a conceptual contradiction and results in extra book-keeping for the institution and occasionally for the students. In competency-based programs with credit-hour systems, for example, students may be certified competent but still not qualify for graduation because they have not accumulated a sufficient number of credits—a predicament that is understandably confusing to the students and the institutions. Double bookkeeping has other artificial ramifications, but the registrar must keep two sets of records, reporting in credit hours to the state and in competencies or other learning-outcome terms on a student's transcript. The arbitrary assignment of credit hours will not work in every situation, nor is it necessarily appropriate, but it has become the solution of least resistance in many instances.

Giving a lump sum of money based on full-time-equivalent students or faculty in a program is a way of providing flexibility in states like New York, where the guidelines currently prohibit spending in any category except the one for which the money was assigned. This partial solution, already available in some states, offers the chance to demonstrate cost effectiveness. In Ohio, for example, funds can be generated through student credit-hour production for faculty but used for paraprofessionals and other less well-credentialled individuals who provide certain learning opportunities as well as faculty but cost considerably less. States that now practice flexible funding should, by all means, continue the activity, and other states should follow their lead. Line budgets are much less appropriate for traditional *and* nontraditional programs grouped together. Again, a kind of double bookkeeping is necessary since funds are received on one basis and spent on another. Lump sums, like arbitrarily assigned credit hours, lead to waste and confusion, but they do offer some flexibility and are potentially cost effective.

Developing baseline data particularly suited to nontraditional programs is a more hopeful and appropriate solution than most of those mentioned above. Since most states with formulas or guidelines use a zero-base or previous-year basis for determining traditional budgets, nontraditional programs need to develop the same kind of baseline information about their costs if they are to compete successfully for funds. Colleges and universities cannot rely on the good will of funding agencies or the assumed worth of their programs, nor can they expect legislators and state administrators to believe that all nontraditional programs warrant support simply because they exist. If time- and place-free programs are to continue to be supported, they must develop data within three years after their initiation to show that they either produce more learning for the same dollars spent for traditional programs, or the same level of learning for fewer dollars.

Far too many nontraditional programs, without making any effort to justify their existence, have complained about the lack of full support. All programs are not effective, and some certainly do not deserve to continue. Although many analyses are underway, some supported by the Fund for the Improvement of Postsecondary Education, no sound basis for demonstrating cost effectiveness has been developed that could be presented to state funding agencies or boards of regents to justify the continued existence of nontraditional programs.

Developing a new formula based on a concept entirely different from credit hours constitutes a very hopeful alternative to traditional funding formulas or guidelines. Robert Toft of College IV, Grand Valley State, recommends developing a funding base determined by how much students learn from the program of instruction. In other words, value-added achievement rates could become the basis for determining how much money an institution receives for educational programs. Such a concept of accountability, based on a direct assessment of the amount of learning acquired rather than on a proxy measure such as the student credit hour, is a revolutionary concept. Unfortunately, the value-added approach is not likely to catch on quickly because of the tremendous threat it poses to those traditional programs that do not know how much their students have learned nor how best to acquire the information if they wanted it.

Another possible basis for a funding formula, developed by Harold Hodgkinson and me under a grant from the Fund for the Improvement of Postsecondary Education, is the Faculty Professional Task Inventory. This instrument lists all the professional behaviors in which faculty engage as part of their workload. Each task on the inventory is weighted, and the number of times a faculty member performs the task is multiplied by the weight for that task. Thus, the total Professional Service Units for a faculty member during a specific time period can be determined. A faculty member's load can be described more accurately by Professional Service Units than by student credit hours since the units portray the total work of faculty and not just what students do. A teacher's Professional Service Units can be divided into his or her salary to determine the cost of each task performed, or any task performed by all members of the faculty can be calculated. This method could provide a new cost base for nontraditional programs.

Program budgeting, for the few states that engage in it, has not presented any major problems for nontraditional programs. Although this method was not proposed as a solution by any of the institutions surveyed, *program budgeting seems to be an appropriate way out of the formula dilemma.* Program budgeting does not interfere with any particular kind of educational program but allows each program to justify its existence and set its priorities through a budget indicating how much money is necessary to carry out each level of activities. Developing program budgeting for large state universities would be extremely complicated, however. Consequently, it will not easily catch on as a solution to the problems of nontraditional programs in such institutions. It could, of course, be combined with other systems of fund allocation or be used exclusively as a basis for justifying individual innovative programs.

Perhaps the most far reaching possibility for solving funding restrictions comes from Norway. That country has developed the equivalent of a *council for innovation that can supersede any and all traditional funding guidelines* for educational programs. Using its own criteria, specially developed for legislative purposes, the council establishes the merits of innovative programs that do not fit into traditional education budgets. This council, recently described by Norwegian educators visiting in the United States, seems to offer each state an ombudsmanlike potential for solving the funding problems of nontraditional programs.

Of all suggestions received from the institutions surveyed, the largest number centered on *changing the formulas or guidelines themselves.* Several different ideas were presented; some may be broadly adopted, although others apply only to the specific situations out of which they arose.

The first suggestion is to build an override into the formula system of every state. Francis Gross's recent study of funding formulas in twenty-five states supports this override. Gross recommends that "provision be made in each state's formula for additional requests supported by objective and subjective data."[5] Such an override could be accommodated either by a weighted base formula for long-term support, or a direct amount for short-term support. Funds would be allocated for planning, program development, implementation, and the cost of determining the baseline data.

Another possibility is to include a percentage for program development as a new category of funding formulas. This suggestion is similar to the override but specially designed for new program development. The results are also similar to those in the override but are accomplished on a sliding scale instead of through a flat amount. No public discussion of formulas has ever considered new programs as a legitimate category. Yet, considering the large number of innovative programs introduced annually in public and private education, adding a percentage of either the base factor or the flat amount to a funding formula for the development of nontraditional programs seems appropriate.

A third recommendation for changing formulas is to establish a full-time-equivalent student base factor, if not already established, and add a special rate for nontraditional programs. By such a device, if a base factor of $1200 per student was allocated, depending upon the level of the program, an additional 10 or 20 percent rate of that base would be added for the initial costs of innovative programs.

Fourth, the base factor per full-time-equivalent student could be changed by allocating an expanded flat amount per full-time student in a new formula category for nontraditional programs. The flat amount in traditional programs might be $1200 for the first two years of undergraduate study and $1500 in nontraditional programs. But this suggestion, by assuming that innovative programs are always more expensive than traditional ones, is poor justification for their continuation.

A fifth alternative would use a zero-base traditional cost standard and add an increment for nontraditional programs. In all states with formulas, base factor, zero-base factor, full-time-equivalent student flat allocation, or percentage allocation is used to

[5]Gross, p. vi.

determine funding. Each could easily be combined with an increment for nontraditional programs.

A sixth approach would be to use a student-faculty contact-hour ratio instead of a credit-hour ratio for determining instructional costs, and then add a percentage for planning, development, implementation, and departmental expenses in addition to faculty salaries. Many formulas incorporate some kind of student-faculty ratio in their design. As pointed out earlier, this ratio is ordinarily based on the student credit hour but could just as well be based on the contact hour that, in modular programs and other individualized activities, would be a more meaningful measure of faculty effort. Empire State College in New York, for example, uses contact hours and designates one contract month of study as equivalent to four credit hours in a traditional system.

A seventh formula modification suggested is to establish a different balance in the formula ratio for nontraditional programs. In New York, for example, the traditional ratio is one full-time-equivalent faculty for every twenty-four full-time-equivalent undergraduates. Empire State originally was placed on a one-to-thirty ratio, which actually reduced the amount of money available for developing programs. This recommendation moves in the opposite direction, urging a lower faculty-student ratio for nontraditional programs until they can justify their existence in a cost-effective manner.

A final solution to problems of aid restriction to colleges for part-time or off-campus students is to change the regulation. Since restrictions were imposed by states and the Veterans Administration to overcome misuses of state and federal funds, any change in the regulations must continue to safeguard against abuses. Requiring regional accreditation for part-time or off-campus programs would still penalize some students and programs but considerably fewer than are now penalized. Or, in lieu of accreditation, *innovative programs desiring state aid or VA benefit eligibility could be required to meet specially developed criteria similar in concept but in not content to accreditation standards.* The state or federal government could then validate and certify programs for eligibility. Such criteria could and should be developed to avoid stifling some of the most promising cost-effective ways of delivering post-secondary education.

Although a substantial majority of respondents indicated

that the formulas, guidelines, and regulations in the states should
be changed, they also were quick to point out that change of that
magnitude ordinarily occurs only when the budget structure becomes intolerable to administrators of traditional collegiate programs. Nontraditional programs usually have to derive their benefits indirectly from the actions of the traditional program officers.
Respondents also noted that the persons who generate nontraditional programs frequently have limited bureaucratic skills, and
this places them at a political disadvantage within their institutions. They may be at the top of the pedagogical order but at the
bottom of the pecking order. Although changing budget formulas
seems to be a good solution, nontraditional program directors
themselves are not likely to be in a position to effect that change.
They must rely on institutional administrators, state budget officers, and state directors of higher education to comprehend the
problems and seek the solutions.

In conclusion, state formulas and guidelines and some federal funding policies clearly are too restrictive and inflexible to
allow nontraditional programs to function effectively. The formulas or guidelines currently used by thirty-three states offer no
incentive to be cost effective since the basis for budgeting is last
year's or this year's actual costs. Some formulas, designed to improve accountability, to increase fairness in programming, and to
provide resources for the most effective programs within a state,
have become a mechanism for defeating those very aims. Thus, the
irony of budget formulas is that they may work against the purposes they were designed to serve. This contradiction results when
formulas fail to be flexible enough to take into account the developmental costs of nontraditional programs, when they fail to
require that innovative as well as traditional programs be based on
more cost-effective concepts than last year's expenditures, and
when colleges that do not pass their costs along to students are
financially penalized because support is based on those charges.

Although innovative time- and place-free programs must be
cost effective to compete in the marketplace of higher education,
they must also be given sufficient funding to develop the skills,
assessment instruments, teaching-learning techniques, and administrative strategies necessary to reduce costs or increase learning
achievement. Implementation costs, operating parallel nontraditional and traditional programs, and research on new ways of

delivering education—all are expensive. If budgeting formulas and guidelines cannot provide for these costs by some legitimate means, then the possibility of developing meaningful alternatives to traditional educational structures is greatly diminished.

Those states that design budget formulas and guidelines are justifiably concerned about being accountable to the public; however, by failing to include provisions that allow developing programs the time and financial support they need in order to justify themselves on any cost-effective basis, states hamper their own long-term educational efficiency and restrict themselves to the continually inflating costs of traditional programs. By supporting the development of sound educational alternatives that someday may prove to be considerably less expensive and more effective, federal and state governments can be more accountable to the populace than they have been in the past. Only by a concerted action of educators, administrators, state budget officers, legislative committees, federal program officers, and chief higher education officers in every state can some satisfactory solutions to restrictive state and federal funding guidelines for nontraditional programs be established.

19

Higher Education Among National Budget Priorities

Carol Van Alstyne

A great debate on financing higher education was launched in 1973, when the Committee for Economic Development and the Carnegie Commission recommended that college tuition be raised and that the added costs be offset by increased aid to needy students. That debate is now broadening to encompass issues relating to the place of higher education among national budget priorities.

One way to assess the current budget priority given to higher education is to look at trends in federal spending and to compare support for higher education with support for other sectors. Total federal support for higher education, both for institutions and students, is slightly more than one-third of the Office of Education budget, less than 3 percent of the entire federal budget, and a mere half percent of the gross national product. After increasing rapidly in the early 1960s, federal expenditures for higher education flattened out between 1968 and 1974; in fact, they were lower in 1974 than in 1968. Estimated budget outlays for fiscal 1975 broke sharply from this no-growth trend, showing an increase of almost 50 percent (including, however, some forward funding into future fiscal years). But the budget for fiscal 1976 incorporated little increase over 1975.

Trends in federal spending for the various components of education and training differ greatly. Elementary and secondary education received two to three times as much as higher education during the mid-1960s, but the increase in support for this sector has slowed down, virtually leveling off since 1972. At the same time, support for manpower training has steadily increased. A decade ago, it was not much larger than support for higher education, but it has grown rapidly and now even exceeds the level of support for elementary and secondary education by a slight amount.

A more trenchant comparison in terms of national priorities is between federal spending for higher education and federal spending for defense. Even though defense spending has taken a decreasing share of the federal budget in recent years, dropping from 44 percent in 1968 to 27 percent in 1976, the average annual increase in the defense budget during that period was $8.3 billion —$900 million more than the *total* 1976 federal budget proposed by the Administration for higher education.

Trends in the federal share of institutional revenues and of student resources offer other indications of where higher education stands among national budget priorities. The proportion of institutional income that came from the federal government peaked at a little over 20 percent in the mid-1950s. During the early 1970s, the proportion decreased considerably, particularly in the private sector, where involvement in graduate education and research was greater. While edging back up from the trough of 1970-1971, the federal share of total institutional revenues still does not approach earlier peaks. The difference has been made up by increases in state support and tuition.

Policy statements on the shift from direct institutional aid to support for students might lead one to expect that the federal contribution to institutional revenues would show up in the form of student tuition. But even after a decade of new student aid programs, the percentage of overall student expenses covered by federal support was lower than it had been thirty years before. In 1947, the GI Bill helped more than one out of every two students enrolled in colleges and universities. It covered 40 percent of the educational expenses—both tuition and living costs—of all students. Yet today, when federal assistance is intended to broaden access, the proportion of direct student expenses covered by federal assistance is less than 30 percent.

Another consideration is that the funds allotted to Office of Education student assistance programs cover two types of "student aid." The first, paid to cover the student's tuition and living expenses, includes Basic Educational Opportunity Grants, College Work-Study, and Supplemental Educational Opportunity Grants. Together with National Direct Student Loans, these programs account for about two-thirds of total Office of Education student aid funds and are subject to annual appropriations limits. The second type of aid consists of funds paid to lenders—interest subsidies, special interest allowances, and coverage of losses caused by defaults or death and disability—to induce them to make loans to students. Thus, the term *student aid* is inconsistently applied. Moreover, this second type differs from the first in another important way: Payment of federal funds to the lenders is obligated under contractual agreement; if not enough funds are appropriated initially, a supplemental request must be made. In 1975, an astounding one-third of the total Office of Education student assistance funds was channeled to lenders. Sharp increases in the funds channeled to lenders without commensurate increases in the overall amounts of student aid requested means that substantially fewer dollars are channeled directly to students. In view of large increases in college costs and expanded eligibility for assistance, individual students may be getting far less real assistance now than they did previously.

State support for higher education is fully twice the level of federal support. Expenditures for higher education often are the largest single item of a state budget, ranging from one-sixth to one-third of the total. Though the proportion for higher education has declined from peak levels in some states, the absolute amount appropriated has increased since 1973 in forty-nine states. Inflation has wiped out about two-thirds of the value of the increase, but even so real dollar support has grown about 10 percent for all states.

Individual institutions may have lost support, however, as states have channeled funds into expanding their public systems (particularly two-year institutions) and into increasing their direct aid to students, or have failed to make up for the erosion of inflation.

Complicating the picture of trends in federal and state support for higher education is the federal revenue-sharing program, initiated in 1972 to distribute $30.2 billion, one-third to states and two-thirds to local governments. Reportedly, large amounts of revenue-sharing dollars are being spent for education, but no precise information is available on whether they are going to the elementary and secondary sector or to higher education and on whether they are being added to regular state tax funds or substituting for these funds, thus permitting states to shift their own funds to other program areas or even to cut state and local taxes.

It is paradoxical that debate on federal aid to institutions often founders on the issue of full accountability for the use of public funds, whereas revenue sharing—which is intended to allow states wide latitude in the use of public funds—is advocated on the opposite grounds: that states are in the best position to know what they need.

On March 6, 1975, the Carnegie Council on Policy Studies in Higher Education issued its first official report, *The Federal Role in Postsecondary Education: Unfinished Business, 1975-1980* (San Francisco: Jossey-Bass). The report calls for the inauguration of several major new programs of federal assistance to higher education. One program is tuition equalization grants to states that would reduce the gap in tuition between private and public institutions. The second is the creation of a self-supporting National Student Loan Bank. The third is financial assistance to large research libraries. The funds required to carry out these recommendations were carefully calculated by the Council to increase federal expenditures for higher education "modestly" from 0.64 percent of the gross national product in 1974-1975 to 0.66 percent in 1979-1980. But the Council failed to deal adequately with the issue of what the national priority for higher education *should* be.

The report seems to imply either that the higher education share should be no larger than it is or that securing a larger share, however justified, is not politically feasible given limited resources and competing demands. Whichever of these premises is operative, it should be explicitly stated and openly debated.

The new proposals in the O'Hara Bill (H.R. 3471) for restructuring student aid also add up to a level of support for students little different from that provided by existing legislation, even though awarded in differing patterns. This bill represents too early and too complete a concession to "budget realities," without considering the question "Can and should higher education rise among national priorities?" I would like here to encourage serious considerations of that question.

Before higher education can press successfully for a higher place among national budget priorities, we will have to do a much better job, first, of making the case and, second, of documenting it. Much conceptual and analytic work will be required to devise improved ways to measure the financial needs of students and of institutions. Student-needs analysis originated as a mechanism for limiting competition among institutions in the award of funds and, more recently, has been used for allocating as equitably as possible the inadequate student aid funds available. Needs analysis has not altogether transcended those origins to become a technique for determining real student need, based on explicit value judgments about reasonable self-help expectations and about the roles of the state and federal governments.

On the institutional side, pleas for increased support are not likely to be persuasive until vast improvements are made in measuring the financial condition of colleges and universities. We need a financial assessment that is equivalent to the bottom line in industry, and the current operating fund surplus or deficit is not an equivalent measure.

In the past, claims that greater support is needed have been based on comparisons with funding in the previous year—an incremental or "more is better" approach. This approach no longer works with increasingly skeptical legislators and program administrators. Relative budget shares for higher education are not adequate measures of priorities at the federal or state level either. Requests must be framed in terms of the resources needed to do specific jobs. We have to look beyond the share of support for higher education—and even beyond the survival of particular institutions—to the balance between the resources available and the missions to be accomplished.

Then we need to take a hard look at the obstacles to making greater claims for support for higher education. One obstacle—one that we have erected ourselves—is our own persecution complex. Critical intellectual ability is highly valued in the academic world; directed inward, self-criticism is productive when used to improve the teaching-learning process and to strengthen the relevance of curricular offerings to current student and community concerns. But overdone, self-criticism turns into a self-destructive paranoia that leads academics to explain complex social phenomena too exclusively in terms of the shortcomings of higher education. For instance, "declining enrollments" are frequently attributed in part to student disaffection with college, to student reassessment of the value of a college degree and its relevance to life goals. But there are two difficulties with this explanation. First, enrollments are not down, they are up, in both the public and the private sectors. The expected demographic contraction of the traditional college-age population will not occur until the early 1980s. Second, enrollments are increasing despite the fact that students are now being asked to pay almost twice as much for a college education as they paid a decade ago. It is amazing that enrollments have not, in fact, declined. When home buying slumps, when automobile sales plummet, when beef consumption drops, the explanation given is not that people no longer like housing or cars or steak but that the prices are too high. Demand for a college education is not absolute but is a function of the prices. Noneconomists need to pay attention to possible economic explanations of enrollment trends and to be skeptical of broadside generalizations about young people's disenchantment with higher education. Economists, however, need to pay attention to the values of education beyond economics.

The same holds true with the assertion that private giving to higher education slumped because private donors were dissatisfied with the ability of academic institutions to govern themselves during the era of student unrest. Actually, year-to-year trends in individual and corporate donations follow (with consistent time lags for the contribution process) almost exactly the trends in net corporate profits. Once again, the paranoid explanation has been too easily accepted.

Another obstacle to raising the priority of higher education is the alleged surplus of college graduates. Ominous reports of college graduates who cannot find jobs related to their education and encounters with taxi-driving Ph.D.s have led some people to raise serious questions about the need to stimulate, at least through public subsidy, even greater college enrollments. The Bureau of the Census projects a doubling of the number of college graduates in the adult population by 1990—from fifteen million to thirty million—raising the population share from 11 percent to 20 percent. Such statistics provoke dismal speculations about the fate of unemployed or underemployed college graduates: hyperextension of graduate education for those with baccalaureates who can't get jobs, and even wild scenarios of social upheaval led by the desperately overeducated.

Priorities for higher education depend fundamentally on what is considered the appropriate size of the higher education sector. According to the standard forecasts, we are moving from a period of excess demand for college graduates to a period of excess supply. This change supposedly will reduce the economic returns to investment in education and consequently reduce the demand for higher education. These projections that demand for higher education will probably decrease are based on human capital theory. But whatever its analytic elegance, this theory is a weak, if not dangerous, basis for formulating public policy with respect to the size of the education sector. Its use for such purposes should be challenged—whether such a challenge leads to conclusions that funding should be decreased or increased.

For one thing, the calculation of the economic returns may not be free of conceptual flaws. Differences in returns attributed to the number of years of education may in fact stem from differences in ability, experience, or motivation, from increased opportunities for on-the-job learning, or from restrictive labor practices. Further, the calculation of returns is subject to measurement errors, particularly when returns to investment in education are compared with returns to investment in physical capital. For instance, our tax structure permits deduction of the expenses necessary to earn income in the case of physical capital but not in the case of human capital; it allows depreciation of the asset value of physical capital but not of human capital; and it allows capital gains treatment of the appreciation of physical capital but not of the income of people who spend years gaining the competence being rewarded. Whatever use can be made of economic rates of return to explain gross enrollment levels, they cannot adequately explain choice of field or of degree earned. The computations grossly overemphasize economic determinants of education as a productive investment and exclude what economists call the consumption value, or what others might call the sheer exhilaration of learning.

Even if the returns could be carefully calculated, allowing them to dictate funding policy might be dangerous. Consider, for instance, the general finding that returns to education investments for employed women are lower than those for employed men. Does this imply that less money should be invested in the education of women and more in the education of men to align their marginal rates of return more closely? Human capital theory does not, by itself, tell us whether the returns flow from characteristics of individuals or from characteristics of the social and economic system.

Calculating the demand for and the supply of college-educated people is the beginning, not the end, of an inquiry about the appropriate size of the education sector. In a democracy, the first question is not how big the education sector should be; rather, it is who decides who gets what opportunities for how much education. Elitist education was used in the past as the social justification for economic inequality. Broadening access to education is now understood to be necessary, even if not sufficient, to reduce the sources of social and economic disparities. To argue that because more education might reduce income disparities, we should therefore have less education is, then, a strange reversion to elitism.

Another obstacle we have to deal with is the inflation and recession which have hit virtually every segment of our economy —and some segments even harder than education. We are told to wait until better times to press for more financial support. Times are tough, and all must do their share of belt-tightening. Even so we must make sure that higher education is not unnecessarily disadvantaged during periods of economic adversity. For instance, President Gerald Ford's energy and economic package involved a surcharge on imported fuel which increased the cost of fuel; that increase was at least partially offset by tax rebates to families and corporations and by grants to state and local governments and federal agencies adversely affected. But the Administration quite literally forgot the nonprofit sector—including colleges and universities—which may be among the largest consumers of energy in a service area and which may pay millions of dollars in energy costs. They were ineligible for any of the rebates, but they had to bear the full brunt of increased energy costs when consumption could be cut no further. Higher education must guard against this kind of oversight.

On the positive side, higher education can be instrumental in carrying out economic policy: for instance, by packaging educational assistance and public service jobs for part-time students/part-time workers, thereby creating opportunities for learning while reducing unemployment, at a considerably smaller cost to the federal government than that for full-time public service jobs or unemployment compensation.

Deep philosophical concerns about the size of the public sector, fear about undue government encroachment on institutional autonomy, and the conviction that colleges and universities must first more effectively manage the resources already at their command undergird the assertion that "the government can't do it all." Unfortunately, that assertion often closes off real discussion of policy alternatives requiring public resources.

Consider an alternative assertion equally meritorious: that higher education should be as advantaged as—or at least no more disadvantaged than—other sectors that claim public support. Thus, the data that the government provides to higher education should be equivalent in scope, quality, and timeliness to the data it provides to agriculture, private industry, and labor. In negotiating contracts to perform research services, educational institutions should be permitted to cover overhead and other expenses at rates giving them at least as much capacity to develop new research projects and to adjust to rapid shifts in funding as is permitted in contracts with business firms. The claims of institutions that special costs associated with providing educational services to disadvantaged students should be offset parallels the claims of lenders that their special costs should be offset; these claims should be given equal weight. And claims that support levels should be adjusted to compensate for the devastating effects of inflation should be recognized as equally legitimate for institutions of higher education as they are, say, for defense contractors.

The higher education community understands very well that the government can't do it all. We are also beginning to understand the realities of the new budgeting process. Previously, authorizing committees simply wrote legislation and left it to others to find the money. Now programs are to be designed within attainable funding levels. It is to be hoped that our new understanding of the budget process will not entail adopting conventionally conservative attitudes toward public spending for human service programs. Perhaps it takes people less familiar with the budget process to try to escalate the level of trade-offs.

What strategies are available for pressing the claims of higher education for greater national attention and support? In our society, resource-allocation strategies operate in three domains: economic, relying on market mechanisms; rational, incorporating planning processes; and political, using persuasion and voting power. Recent policy proposals in higher education have tended to focus exclusively on market mechanisms in the economic domain, but that approach is likely to be less effective than conscious action in all three domains.

In order to increase total resources available for higher education and to enhance the role of the market in determining the size and composition of the higher education sector, the Newman Task Force, the Committee for Economic Development, and the Carnegie Commission proposed to raise tuitions and increase direct student assistance. But the market—an idealized abstraction with real-world imperfections—is hardly better at making big decisions than little decisions and is certainly not any more adequate in determining the major priorities for education than it is, say, in determining those for national security.

It is not certain that relying on market mechanisms would assure a rich diversity of offerings and a wide variety of real educational choices from which well-informed students might select. On the contrary, there is a serious risk that institutions—fearful that wrong decisions about specialization may threaten their survival—will move in the direction of greater similarity rather than greater diversity, thus broadening the educational offerings at individual institutions but narrowing them systemwide. The market approach might result in duplicated curricular offerings and delivery options and thus even result in higher costs for students than a planned and coordinated educational system would. And improving the operation of educational market mechanisms is not the only, or even the best, strategy for learning about and responding to the educational preferences of students.

Planning the allocation of resources is generally an under-developed art in education, with only a few outstanding exceptions in individual states and institutions. Vast improvements in the quality and timeliness of data available, as well as significant advances in the development of policy analysis and operating management models can greatly enhance our ability to plan in higher education. At the same time, we must develop a working understanding of both the short-term and long-term relationships between overall economic activity and activity in higher education.

As for political strategies, education associations and institutions are forbidden by law from engaging in outright political activity on pain of losing their tax-exempt status. That does not, however, prohibit such organizations from underscoring the critical importance of politics to the future of higher education. Invited testimony by educators about the anticipated impact of alternative legislative proposals on higher education can be powerfully influential.

Legislative committee members and staff are willing to listen to the concerns of their higher education constituents, and they welcome solid information, succinctly summarized in a usable form. Genius is required on the part of educators, however, to anticipate the issues to be debated far enough in advance to have the relevant information ready in time.

Educational associations, state administrators, individual institutions, faculty, and students are gaining increasing political awareness and sophistication and are becoming more and more knowledgeable about political structures, processes, and personalities. Talk is even heard in meetings of educators about building constituencies.

Enormous progress has been made recently in developing mutual understanding that the many segments of education have a shared destiny and that conflicts among those segments are ultimately counterproductive. As a result, most major differences are now resolved before reaching state and federal legislative chambers, whereas in earlier years one segment could often be pitted against another to the detriment of both. Attempts are now being made to reach a consensus and present a united front on policy preferences and budget priorities. Private institutions, for example, were previously among the prime advocates of raising tuitions at public institutions. They have reversed their stance as an act of statesmanship since they recognized that the earlier position would pit them against public institutions. Even further, they have generously endorsed the practice of public institutions' soliciting private voluntary contributions, a major source of revenue to the private institutions. The other half of the implied bargain is that public institutions will now actively promote the appeals of private institutions for increased public support.

People who forecast differing prospects for the future support of higher education—for the place of higher education among national budget priorities—do not, in general, differ markedly in the way they characterize the current financial situation. But they do differ radically in their assessment of what is possible in the academic, economic, and political spheres. The future realities may be as harsh as the darkest forecasts, but we should not start out with such an assumption. If the first step into the future is to limit our horizons, to scale down our expectations, to narrow our choices to feasible but pinched alternatives, we will have taken a realistic course. But there is a more fully responsible course, toward a grander vision, truer to our own beliefs in the values of higher education. We have, I believe, only begun our pursuit of this course.

Creative
Planning

Willard F. Enteman

The Deputy Commissioner of Education of New York State, Ted Hollander, is a person whose acquired and intuitive understanding of higher education I admire greatly. Occasionally, he goes around the state giving what he calls a "gloom and doom" speech. It is filled with careful, precise, and accurate comments about the demographic future of New York with respect to the age group that has traditionally made up the student population. For institutions that have done no planning or only the most superficial planning, the speech is indeed a message of gloom and doom. Most educators have heard this message, or one like it, at one time or another. In fact, my concern is not that people have not heard and reacted to it, but that many may have overreacted to it.

Hollander's message for higher education has much in common with the Club of Rome's famous "limits to growth" message dealing with the problems of advanced industrial societies. Both messages are written in a special context that assumes that many or most people in responsible positions have a euphoric and naive vision about the possibilities for endless growth. Of course, many people have been remarkably naive about the future of advanced industrial societies in general and about the future of higher education within those societies. But a growing number of people are extremely sensitive to the issues pointed out by Ted Hollander and others—so sensitive, in fact, that their reaction often takes the form of despair.

If depression and resignation were the appropriate responses to these warnings about the future, then I suppose I would join those who would prefer to ignore or refute them. In my interpretation, however, the messages should call forth our best energies, for they indicate the kinds of problems our institutions will have to deal with in order to thrive in the future.

The euphoria of the 1960s, which characterized so many leaders of higher education, has been shattered by reality. However, we should not replace naive optimism with an equally naive pessimism. What we should do seems obvious: stop being naive. Both the optimism of the 1960s and pessimism of the early 1970s suffered from a lack of careful planning. There is some logic to the current reluctance to plan for the future. After all, if one's case really is terminal, it seems senseless to spend much time talking about long-term strategies. There is a crisis of dollars and a crisis of enrollment for institutions dependent on the conventional student age group. Of that there can be little doubt. However, the crisis that concerns me most is the crisis of imagination and courage. Unless that crisis is solved, "doomsday" may become a self-fulfilling prophecy. The swing in emotional response from the 1960s to the early 1970s is understandable since the intellectual base was shallow in both periods. If we can deepen and strengthen the intellectual base, a genuinely positive attitude may be substituted for mere sentimentalism.

Some education leaders hope to avoid the problems of the 1970s and 1980s, and probably of the 1990s, by essentially reactive and habitual devices. In the private sector, habitual reaction leads institutions to raise tuitions, reduce financial aids, curtail or eliminate programs, curb the growth of libraries, or dismiss faculty and staff. Another, somewhat more sophisticated, habitual response is to put greater effort into increasing "external" funding. This means intensifying work on fund drives and persuading government agencies to make more significant financial contributions. For some institutions, these habitual responses may be appropriate. For some, substantial enrollment growth can still be projected. However, considered collectively, institutions cannot realistically project such enrollment growth. Similarly, a growth in external funding can be projected for some institutions, but such projections are not realistic for most institutions under current and expected conditions. The point here is not that the quest for increased external funding or increased youth enrollment is wrong, but that all institutions—public and private—should also develop alternate plans. An institution should get its house in order through careful and serious planning. Incidentally, one of the side benefits of planning is that it can help generate external funding. Foundations, government agencies, and individual philanthropists are less and less content with what appears to them to be carefree and unrealistic leadership in higher education.

The word *accountability* has been used almost as much in our realm as *retrenchment* and *steady state*. Real administrators, of course, have always been accountable. The proper issue is not whether higher education shall be accountable, but to whom. Private colleges remain accountable to their boards and to students, who expect responsiveness to their needs. The addition of other sources of bureaucratic accountability may reassure some government agencies but, as public institutions know, will dampen the spirit of pluralism. In the context of retrenchment, added levels of accountability will conclusively remove control and room for initiative from the hands of the institution. Thus, private colleges and universities will have to respond and not just react to market forces in the next few decades. If they cannot show through careful planning that they are in control and appropriately accountable, they may well deserve the extra controls imposed on them.

Partial planning will not be adequate. Such planning, as it is beginning to be employed in private institutions, is related almost exclusively to internal resource allocation and administrative control mechanisms. Recent examples are the management information and management by objectives systems borrowed from industry. These techniques can easily turn institutions into efficient hierarchical bureaucracies in which the price and control of every program is known, but the value and educational merit of none are considered. An appropriate and thorough planning process must include careful market analysis, something which is almost totally lacking in higher education. Consider pricing, for example. Pricing is only one factor in total market plans, but it is the one which has received the most discussion. Private institutions fear they are pricing themselves out of the market, but what evidence do we have on price elasticity? Virtually none. What else do we know about our markets? Very little.

The potential markets for higher education include not only students, but also potential donors, friends, associates, and the public at large. There are markets that have not been tapped and there are undertapped markets. As individual institutions find their own particular markets, they can better orientate themselves to them and plot alternative courses and choose the most appropriate one. Herein lies ground for optimism. Careful, thorough planning is a positive response to the condition of retrenchment. Failing to plan may bring about the worst fears of the pessimists.

The desire to survive is strong in any institution. However, colleges and universities, perhaps more than any other social organizations, should never adopt a "survival-at-all-costs" orientation. Their business is not organizational survival, but educational service. If a rational analysis shows that some educational services are either not needed or not sufficiently appreciated, the response should be to close the operations with dignity while the institution is still in control. If institutions go to bankruptcy court, let them do so in the name of educational principles, not in the name of survival. If some colleges or universities must close—and it seems probable some must—let them make that decision creatively and rationally. At least such action will demonstrate the intellectual integrity for which they have stood.

All too often, the most important result of good planning is considered to be a set of documents. The documents may project enrollment figures, program costs, external funding, curricular reform, faculty development, building plans, and more; they may take into account the total operations of the university. What is ultimately important in creative planning, however, is not the documents themselves but the process of planning. The documents should come as a by-product, albeit an important and necessary one.

There are several reasons for arguing in favor of the process rather than the product. The first is related to campus politics. Experienced administrators have learned that consulting with faculty and other groups on decisions after the fact can often take more time and be more destructive than consulting with them before the fact. I recognize that there are important exceptions to this generalization. Sometimes important decisions have to be made without consultation because consultation would either lead to no decision at all or to a reaction that would prevent the decision from being implemented. In most cases, however, consultation is possible and necessary. The issue is not *whether* the decision maker should consult, but *when*. By anticipating problems before they emerge, the planning process permits consultation before decisions are made.

There is a second reason for emphasizing planning as a process: when planning is sufficiently developed, making new plans and adjusting old ones in light of new evidence is not as difficult as it would be otherwise. When all attention is focused on conclusions or on bottom line decisions, then all the effort that went into the original decision-making process must be regenerated for new adjustments or changes. But if planning is recognized as a process and not the mere production of plans, then the evidence and intelligence that have gone into the plans should be readily available for necessary adjustments.

A third reason is that colleges and universities are complex and *must* plan far ahead. For example, at my own institution, Union College, more than 50 percent of the operating budget is committed to employee contracts of no less than one year. Another 10 percent goes to debt service expense and 15 to 20 percent goes to other legally fixed annual costs. Consequently, on any particular date, about 80 percent of the budget for the next year is legally fixed. This does not even take into account other commitments of a binding nature. I suppose one can conceive of adding no materials to the library, of supplying no science laboratories, and of eliminating sabbaticals on less than one year's notice. One can conceive of such things, but, speaking practically, one cannot really imagine putting them into effect. Thus, on a one-year planning basis, we face a situation in which more than 90 percent of the budget is locked up and there is virtually no flexibility. In such a situation, planning must be reactive rather than creative. However, if one moves ahead two, three, or four years, considerably more legal and moral flexibility is possible. Further, proper consultation is possible among administrators, faculty, students, and others. Creative planning should involve goal setting for the various functional areas of the institution. If program administrators have participated in setting the objectives, and if they can see how those objectives are related to the overall plans of the institution, their commitment to achieving them will be greater.

Finally, the fourth reason for stressing process instead of product is the tendency both on campus and off to look at near-term irritations, not long-term possibilities. Insofar as planning emphasizes the production of plans, then that production is transformed into a near-term irritation. It becomes an irritant that competes alongside other irritants. Being sure that a professor's blackboard is wiped competes with considerations of needed curricular reform. Resolving a dispute between roommates competes with consideration of what kind of students the college should seek and how it should transform them. Parking, football, parietal rules—the litany is familiar to all and will compete with and drive out proper planning unless that planning is built into the institution and structured as a process. On this score, the board of trustees of an institution can be of great help. The board can achieve a distance from the daily irritants, and it can insist on evidence to support the planning process. That evidence should not be merely the presentation of plans, but the development and maintenance of a continual process which, on appropriate occasions, produces plans.

The suggestions I make about creative planning are not without their own problems. The first has to do with the unreliability of longer term projections. The further into the future we plan, the less reliable the plans. Defeatists like to ask what our estimated energy costs for this year would have looked like on the basis of a 1971 projection, but we must refuse to accept the implication that we should not plan and should not project. The more insecure and unreliable the future is, the more we must plan for it. If we do otherwise, the environment will control us completely. One way to deal with the unreliability problem is to develop an agreed upon reliability index (on a 0-1 basis) and multiply that by planned needs for the future. Actual commitments would then be made only to the extent allowed by the multiplication product. Future plans would be refined as they became more nearly current and as reliability increased. Perhaps there are other methods that could deal with this problem better; I am not aware of any, but I would be glad to aid the search for them.

A second and perhaps more serious problem is identifying the person or persons who are to be primarily responsible for the planning process. Enough has been said about consultation already to indicate that when planning is seen as essentially a process, wide and complete consultation should be sought. However, who should do the seeking? Who should lead the process and be responsible for its development? In my experience with colleges and universities, either planning is inadequate or it is done in an office of institutional research or institutional planning. We have already considered problems associated with inadequate or nonexistent plans. The problems associated with having planning done in specially designated offices may not be as obvious, but they may be more crucial. The institution with no serious long-range planning process cannot pretend it has one, and it may be brought to understand its deficiencies. However, the institution that has created a special office, and has even devoted some of its hard-earned resources to such an office, may well fool itself into thinking something important has been accomplished. The notion that primary responsibility for planning can be delegated away from the chief administrative officers is caused by thinking mistakenly that the purpose of planning is the production of plans. Special planning offices often cause the process to lose its credibility; when that happens, implementing the product becomes practically impossible.

The chief administrative officers of a university should consider planning a major aspect of their jobs, and they must be prepared to engage continually in the process—such as setting priorities and making inevitable trade-offs. They must not shove their responsibilities onto special offices or subordinates, even though participation by all is crucial if the planning is to be seen as a process. Authority for implementing plans must be shared, and the other officers of the institution must—as a result of the planning—must be given clear objective goals that they are to meet. To whatever extent possible and reasonable, such goals should be measurable so that their attainment can be identified and rewarded.

In examining credentials before hiring a new president, provost, or dean, we very rarely inquire about that person's planning skills. Rather, we call on the candidate to provide evidence of considerable intellectual and scholarly ability. Ironically, it is often the on-campus constituencies, especially faculty, who insist so strongly on such credentials. Trustees and alumni, where they are not deferential to faculty, are often less concerned. Yet once appointed, the new officers are expected to demonstrate competent skills of persuasion, tact, management, and the like. If planning was recognized as a major responsibility of top administrative posts, leadership qualities could be more clearly defined and more properly challenged than they are now.

Some crucial problems appear so large or so indigenous to the institution itself that resolution seems hopeless. Consider, for example, issues related to general morale or previously committed resources or—a popular one currently—tenure. Such problems may appear to be bigger than all of us, but after they are identified, planning can develop. But because creative planning is solution-oriented and not problem-oriented, the process requires that problems be identified in such a way that they are capable of solution. One strategy is to state intermediate objectives and to commit the institution to meeting those objectives, for then progress toward solving the larger problem can be identified and measured. I realize that the whole problem may be greater than the sum of its parts and that solution-by-parts may not solve the whole. However, that notion, which may again lead to a do-nothing negativism, also has a counterpart: the solution of the whole may emerge from the solution of each part.

A final problem in planning is that elaborate plans may discourage initiative. If the faculty member or administrator who develops a good innovative idea must wait four or five years before it can be integrated into the planning process, he or she may well be discouraged from pursuing it. The problem is indeed serious, but it can be dealt with by planning so that at least some innovative projects will be accepted and funded. The funding should be accompanied by appropriate controls, and the funded project should meet measurable interim objectives. Even in the most optimistic planning process, it will be difficult to budget innovative programs, but innovation is as indispensable to higher education as any other program; its cost must be borne.

The point may be made that in order to create responses to retrenchment, the power of positive thinking must be grounded in the power of positive planning. Positive planning provides the only device by which we can gain reasonable control over our future. If colleges and universities with their impressive intellectual resources cannot solve their problems, then pessimism is indeed justified. However, I am convinced that creative planning, if properly carried out, will be rewarded.

❧ 21 ❧

Citizens' Bill of Educational Entitlement

Clifton R. Wharton, Jr.

Like education at all levels, higher education is both a private investment and a public investment. As such, it brings both private and public returns. For the individual, higher education may make possible a higher material standard of living, a more stimulating and satisfying career, and an ability to appreciate and grow through exposure to the wealth of our intellectual and cultural heritage. For society, the returns of higher education take equally diverse forms: the improvement of life through basic and applied research, manpower training, the creation of a more affluent tax base, and direct public service efforts by colleges and universities.

In terms of social policy, governmental subsidy of higher education has been justified traditionally by reference to the public benefit derived therefrom. Higher education has been correctly viewed as an investment in human potential. The original rationale for government subsidization of higher education was and continues to be sound: an educated citizenry contributes to the common good.

The Morrill Act of 1862 was perhaps the prototype of federal recognition of the interdependence of the individual and social benefits of postsecondary learning. In establishing the land-grant colleges and universities, the authors of the Morrill Act created a system destined to become an outstanding international educational model.

During the last three decades, the federal role in public higher education has expanded tremendously. Following World War II, the G.I. Bill became, in a sense, the first citizens' bill of educational entitlement, even though its benefits were only extended to veterans and not to the public at large. The creation of the National Science Foundation in 1950 institutionalized previously ad hoc relationships among government, higher education, and the scientific community and testified to the social worth of the research and research training capacities of higher education. Other milestones included the National Defense Education Act of 1958, the Higher Education Academic Facilities Construction Act of 1963, the Higher Education Amendments and the Health Manpower Act of 1968, and the largely unfunded Higher Education Amendments of 1972.

As one looks at the awesome array of federal legislation, however, two striking features should be noted: first, the concentration on need rather than on entitlement; and second, a dramatic shift in the pattern of funding away from institutional support toward student support. In relation to the first point, I remain fully committed to the provision of financial aid based upon need —no one can dispute its value for improving access to higher education. But in the process of concentrating on need, we have tended to lose sight of the more basic issue of entitlement to education as a fundamental right of all citizens. In relation to the second point, I am not fully committed to the shift toward student support. We have tended to forget that low tuition based on strong institutional aid is an alternative method of achieving the goal of improved access. Certainly such an approach is highly complementary to need-based student aid.

Both trends have been further compounded by a notable increase in the cost burdens borne by students and their parents. In 1960, for example, a Michigan resident student bore 21 percent of the direct cost of an education at Michigan State University; by 1970, the percentage had increased to 30 percent. The basic fact is that higher education costs have been rising at a rate of nearly 20 percent per year[1] without comparable increases in public and private support. Under the circumstances, tuition increases have become the major resource for institutional survival. The result has been a dramatic increase in tuition at both public and private institutions and a notable shift toward a greater student share of the cost burden.

Students have had to assume a greater share of the costs of higher education partly because universities have been unable to offset cost increases by greater productivity. Although it is true that efficiency has improved over the years, sometimes with corresponding declines in quality, I strongly suspect that we are close to a ceiling with current technology. Hereafter, most gains in productivity will exact a price in terms of unacceptable reductions in quality. Not long ago, I pointed out that "The search for ever greater and greater increases in productivity can best be put into proper perspective by contrasting pictures of two extremes. Take first the image of a teacher on one end of a log with a student on the other end, then contrast it with the image of our freshman class of 7000 sitting in our football stadium while one lonely professor stands at the fifty-yard line in front of a microphone. The former represents the ancient notion of teaching; the latter would be a demonstration of extremely high productivity—assuming that it were effective.

"The choice between these two educational models, as well as among the many idealized models, depends on a delicate and subjective balancing of educational philosophy and economic effi-

---

[1] Larry L. Leslie, *A Case for Low Tuition*, speech to meeting of Regional/Branch Campus Deans, Rice Lake, Wisconsin, June 1974; revised November 1974, Center for Study of Higher Education, Pennsylvania State University, occasional paper.

ciency. I often wonder whether as a matter of public policy the ever-growing press for greater productivity is not leading us to the football stadium classroom. Is this what the students, their parents, or the tax-paying citizens really want? From the criticism I hear, I doubt it."[2]

As social institutions depending mainly on people to provide their services, and with fairly fixed production techniques, universities have been especially vulnerable to the current economic malaise. Inflation and skyrocketing energy costs have undercut every postsecondary institution in the United States. Even for public colleges and universities, state appropriations are rarely adequate to prevent tuition increases. A few years ago the Michigan state legislature adopted a policy of funding only its proportionate share of any budgetary increases granted. If, for example, the legislature determines that a 6 percent raise in the university operating budget is proper, it might appropriate only 4 percent as its proportionate share. As a result, programs must be curtailed or tuition increased, or both. The Michigan policy has virtually dictated lockstep increases in tuition. The problem will be compounded if the legislature refuses to recognize or support cost increases that are politically unattractive, but that are practically or legally unavoidable. It is unlikely that state allocations will halt, much less reverse, the upward trend in tuition costs.

For private colleges and universities, the situation is even more acute. The increase in costs at private universities is rapidly becoming a national epidemic. Among the recently announced tuition increases: Harvard from $3400 to $3740 in 1975-1976; MIT from $3350 to $3700; and Yale from $3650 to $4050. As tuitions inexorably rise and disposable real income at least temporarily declines, students and parents are not only asking whether a college education continues to offer its long-claimed economic rewards but also whether the student can afford to attend college at all.

Is it time, then, for a citizens' bill of educational entitlement? My answer is *yes*—and in my view the federal government must assume a new and more active role in subsidizing the entitlement.

[2] Clifton R. Wharton, Jr., *The State of the University: Hard Times, Hard Choices*, Address to Michigan State University, February 20, 1975.

The Carnegie Council on Policy Studies in Higher Education has released its recommendations for expanding the federal role in higher education. As vice chairman of the council, I heartily endorse the proposals, but they deal largely with such devices as tuition equalization grants to enhance enrollments at private colleges and universities, improved student loan plans, and new or expanded programs of federal aid directly to institutions. These steps, though necessary, are not sufficient. I disagree with the recommendation of the earlier Carnegie Commission on Higher Education (not to be confused with the new Carnegie Council) that individual students or their families should bear an increasingly greater portion of the costs of postsecondary education. It seems to me that the primary objective of any citizens' bill of educational entitlement should be to move once more toward a long-standing ideal of American education: low-cost or no-cost postsecondary schooling similar to that currently available at the primary and secondary school levels.

What might be the outline of a hypothetical federal bill of educational entitlement? First, every high school graduate who is a U.S. citizen would be eligible (contingent on admission to an accredited postsecondary institution) for a specific federal dollar entitlement per year up to a maximum of four years of full-time study within a ten-year period immediately following graduation. For adults who had not completed high school, the initial ten-year eligibility period would commence upon completion of diploma, General Educational Development, or alternate college-admission requirements. I would set the dollar amount at about one-fourth the average cost of current per capita state subsidies to state institutions; for example, a total per capita subsidy of $1500 would mean a federal entitlement of $375.[3] What would be the cost of a citizens' bill of educational entitlement? From materials developed by the Carnegie Commission on Higher Education, it can be estimated that total full-time-equivalent undergraduate enrollments at public and private institutions will top seven million in

[3]This sum has been deliberately chosen to match the proposed tuition equalization grants recommended by the recent Carnegie Council report. See Carnegie Council on Policy Studies in Higher Education, *The Federal Role in Postsecondary Education: Unfinished Business, 1975-1980* (San Francisco: Jossey-Bass, 1975).

1975-1976.[4] At $375 per person, the federal share of expenses would run about $2.6 billion.

Second, after the initial ten-year period, the individual would acquire additional educational entitlement benefits for every year he or she paid federal income tax or met the requirements for federal negative income tax assistance. Again, benefits would accrue up to a maximum of four years of full-time schooling in a ten-year period. Such a provision would be important for professional and graduate training and especially for those who feel a growing need to follow lifelong educational patterns.

Third, a citizen's educational entitlement could be used at any accredited public or private postsecondary institution in the United States and its territorial possessions.

Fourth, the federal entitlement would apply regardless of need. I concur with those who object to proposals that would result in a free public service for some and a high tuition for others. Where students are entitled to federally funded financial aid based upon need, the entitlement would serve as the initial base of an aid package. But the proposal should be designed so as to preclude any reduction in any existing, additional student aid awarded currently by individual states, territories, or institutions. Similarly, the existence of private scholarship and grant programs should not affect the level of entitlement due an individual under federal rules of eligibility.

My rationale for the foregoing approach is based on two assumptions. First, there are growing social returns from education. Lack of adequate education for inner city residents, for example, imposes major social costs through higher crime and welfare rates. Eliminating or reducing such problems through the aid of a federal program would constitute a significant social benefit. Still since there is also a private or personal return from education, we are justified in expecting students to bear a proper share of the cost burden.

Second, interstate residential mobility will increase. This means that the investment one state makes in higher education might result in social benefits for another state. Some states might

[4]Carnegie Commission on Higher Education, Seymour E. Harris, ed., *A Statistical Portrait of Higher Education* (New York: McGraw-Hill, 1972).

even experience net gains at the expense of others. A federal program would help to equalize the educational investment and the benefits accrued therefrom. Of course, since many graduates will continue to reside in the state where they were educated, states should continue their preponderant role in subsidizing higher education. Again, the federal government should not bear the costs alone.

Any move in the direction of a bill of educational entitlement must recognize potential problems, such as the issue of institutional aid versus direct aid to students and the closely related issue of "educational consumerism." The shift toward students paying a larger and larger proportion of the total cost of education has inevitably increased the pressures of educational or student consumerism. As consumers, students enter the academic market and decide at which store (college or university) to shop and what items (courses) to buy. Traditionally, however, student choices have exerted little influence on the activities of a college or university and the allocation of its resources. Institutions have rationalized that the dollars students spend do not cover the full costs of the educational service that they receive. Private universities rely primarily on endowment funds and private gifts to make up the difference; public institutions rely on tax funds from the public sector.

If educational consumerism becomes excessive, it will have a dangerous impact on the allocation of educational resources and investment choices in higher education. The U.S. system of higher education combines elements of a competitive market attracting private investors with elements of public subsidy and control. The market works best in allocating or directing the use of resources when private costs and benefits coincide closely with social costs and benefits. But if students must pay the full or preponderant cost of their degrees, their economic decisions will reflect only personal needs, not those of society. Educational investments that do not provide a personal return will often be ignored. The consequence would be a less than socially desirable level of investment in certain key areas of higher education. The market approach, reflecting the substantial difference between private and social cost-benefit relationships, not only would result in a poor total allocation of resources to higher education but also within the educational system.

Increased educational consumerism would also result in the reduction of the number of courses and subjects that offer high social benefits but little potential for large private earnings. For example, the cost of educating a researcher in pure science is about the same as that of an applied scientist, but the expected incomes for each tend to be quite different because they enter different occupations and industries. This income differential holds true even though the discoveries of the pure scientist, often unpredictable, can have enormous social and economic benefits to the public and even though the scientist rarely derives major personal financial gain from these discoveries. Thus, we can expect that if students are required to bear a greater and greater share of the costs of an expensive course of study, careers will be chosen in those occupations where the graduates can earn high incomes. Students will avoid those careers with the greatest divergence between social and private benefits and seek those with the least divergence. In a system completely dominated by the concept of education as a private good, those areas of knowledge with high potential for social benefits would be ignored. What would happen to the humanistic tradition of American education under such a system?

Another problem is that the current pattern of fees and tuition at most universities and colleges does not take full account of the variation in costs of different courses of study. As the costs of education have increased, the cost gap between certain fields has grown, forcing more widespread pricing differentials. As student control over the funding of higher education increases, we will increasingly and inevitably hear complaints from those students who feel that their fees are higher than they should be and contain hidden subsidies for their classmates in high-cost curricula. Students in English literature or in elementary education will object to their fees and tuition being used to subsidize the higher costs of students in medicine or in low-energy physics. Thus, educational consumerism will lead to tuition charges that more accurately reflect true curricular costs—a trend that may seriously affect the way students choose their majors. Consumerism could also bring pressure on institutions to budget each college, school, or even curriculum according to the revenue it raises. The university and the curriculum, already badly fragmented, would tend to become even more fragmented. Multidisciplinary and interdisciplinary work would become increasingly difficult. Departmental rivalries and jealousies would be further aggravated. Most serious, disciplinary isolationism would become endemic at the very moment when the problems that desperately need solution in our society do not respect traditional disciplinary boundaries.

The impact on research and public service activities would be equally severe. Universities do more than teach students and produce graduates. They also conduct research and engage in public service activities—both of which benefit society. These activities deserve public support in their own right. But many students and taxpayers do not realize that these activities are highly complementary to the teaching function of a university. The discovery of new knowledge through research and experimentation, whether in a laboratory or in a community extension center, is absolutely essential for the continued vitality of the teaching process. The scope and dimension of human knowledge is an ever-changing and ever-expanding aggregation. Failure to support and nourish these activities would quickly lead to the virtual demise of any meaningful teaching function. In a university completely or predominantly supported by student purchases of services, it is most likely that students, wanting to get the most for their money, would demand the undivided attention of the faculty. Even though scholarship and public service experiences tend to enrich future performance, students are most interested in current performance.

Student preferences and competition among colleges will and should affect the nature of the educational product, of course. I am completely convinced that there must be greater responsiveness to the educational concerns and needs of students; such developments are welcome and long overdue. But I would argue strongly that any citizens' bill of entitlement must be accompanied by a well funded program of direct institutional aid. Undoubtedly, a bill of entitlement would dramatically increase the demand for educational access. In a public university, what the student pays in tuition and fees represents about a third of the actual cost of his or her education. Thus, direct aid to students tends to increase the demand upon educational facilities without corresponding support for strengthening and improving the educational output. If funded, the Higher Education Amendments of 1972 would, at least initially, offset increased institutional costs. But that still would not provide enough institutional aid. Any bill of entitlement would have to plan for institutional aid grants as a response to the expanded demand for access as well as to offset the undesired consequences of excessive educational consumerism.

Financing higher education is one of the most critical current issues in American society. Present circumstances convince me that the answer to the question, "Is it time for a citizens' bill of educational entitlement?" should be a resounding "Yes." At the same time, however, we cannot expect such an innovation to provide a panacea for all our ills. In particular, in our search for strategies we must not rush headlong into fads and foibles whose surface attractions mask hidden defects.

We do need a citizens' bill of educational entitlement, but we do not need the abuses of excessive educational consumerism. And we must not assume that direct federal aid to individuals will eliminate the need for federal and state aid to institutions. We must face the problem of financing higher education in all its complexities. An oversimplified approach can only lead to a market-oriented educational system rather than to a system built on excellence and on the desire to extend the frontiers of knowledge, serve the community, and preserve humane values. The loss of any of those would be an irreparable blow to institutions of higher education, students, and the public.

Index